Market Segmentation

MARKETING FOR MANAGERS

This new series provides a set of workbooks focusing on key marketing techniques to help the reader develop expertise in marketing planning and management. Each title presents the central issues around each topic, including:

- a framework in which to start applying these skills;
- self-assessment exercises;
- tool kit of guidelines to improve the performance of the company or department.

Areas covered include segmentation, forecasting, customer service and marketing research. By using these workbooks the reader can analyse particular situations and develop suitable strategies in order to improve the performance of the company or department.

Already published in the series:

Auditing Your Customer Service: John Leppard and Liz Molyneux

Market Segmentation

A step-by-step guide to profitable new business

Michael J. Croft

ROUTLEDGE

London and New York

[redacted]

First published 1994
by Routledge
11 New Fetter Lane, London EC4P 4EE

Simultaneously published in the USA and Canada
by Routledge
29 West 35th Street, New York, NY 10001

Typeset in Times by Solidus (Bristol) Limited
Printed and bound in Great Britain by
Biddles Ltd, Guildford and King's Lynn

British Library Cataloguing in Publication Data

A catalogue reference for this book is available from the British Library.

Library of Congress Cataloging in Publication Data

A catalogue record for this book has been requested.

ISBN 0–415–09736–3

[redacted]

Contents

Figures

Tables

Preface

Much of the theory of market segmentation is appreciated and understood by marketers, and yet it remains one of the more difficult marketing concepts to turn into profitable reality. This book provides an essential guideline to both the theory and the practical application of market segmentation. It covers the definition and benefits of the concept, and explains the processes and techniques that will ensure its successful use in any market. The book also stresses the value of market segmentation to the marketing planning process, as well as to subsequent marketing programmes, and thus it covers many of the wider issues that sometimes cause problems in the implementation of the concept.

The book is aimed at those who have a basic understanding of the theory and practice of marketing, and whilst it includes many different aspects of the subject, it is by no means intended to be a general marketing textbook. For example, the book includes a variety of market research techniques, and the reader may wish to consult more specialist texts to supplement the methodologies I have covered. However, it will be quickly appreciated that market segmentation is so crucial to successful marketing practice that many of these other techniques can be considered as almost a refinement to what should be a central philosophy of doing business.

The approach I have taken follows essentially a 'how to do' format, with different chapters for each of the key steps in the market segmentation process. Each step is described with illustrations that the reader can readily adopt as proformas and, where commercial sensitivities have allowed, I have also included some actual examples for added clarity. The examples and illustrations reflect a slight bias towards industrial markets, in part to counter the usual predominance of consumer market examples in texts on this subject.

At the end of each chapter there is a summary of the key actions for each step, together with a reminder of some of the main points to consider. The overall process is then summarized in chart form at the end of the book. Thus the style of the book is very much one of a workbook, allowing the reader the opportunity to apply the concept of market segmentation as they read.

I believe my approach is unique in offering both a practical and logical guide to delivering profitable new business, and it is an approach that has been shown to work in different types of organisations, and in different markets.

Acknowledgements

I would like to acknowledge helpful comments on the final draft of this book from Professor Malcolm McDonald and Richard Yallop, and also their kind permission to adapt some illustrations and concepts developed at the Cranfield Marketing Planning Centre. I would also like to thank Nigel Thacker, who gave a very useful evaluation of the draft in terms of its value to practising managers.

My overriding debt though is to my wife, Samantha, to whom this book is dedicated.

Michael J. Croft

Introduction

We begin with a look at the theory of market segmentation, and then examine the importance and the benefits of the concept to the marketer, before going on to introduce the step-by-step process that forms the outline of subsequent chapters.

WHAT IS MARKET SEGMENTATION?

A market is simply a group of users with similar needs. It follows from this that a market consists of subgroups, or segments, containing users with slightly different needs to those of other segments. For example, the market for hand tools includes DIY, industrial and professional users. The DIY segment can be subdivided further into enthusiasts, once-in-a-lifetime buyers, gift purchasers, and so on. Whilst they may not be immediately apparent, every market is made up of a myriad of such segments.

Market segmentation is therefore the process of identifying different groups of users within a market who could possibly be targeted with separate products or marketing programmes. The concept has its origins in early economic theory, where it has long been established that demand is linked to the level of competition and to pricing, but it was Smith (1956) who first extended the link to user differences.

WHY IS IT IMPORTANT?

The idea of dividing up a market into homogeneous segments and targeting each with a distinct product and/or message, is now at the heart of marketing theory.

Marketing is concerned with identifying and satisfying user

Figure 0.1 Satisfying user needs – the choice

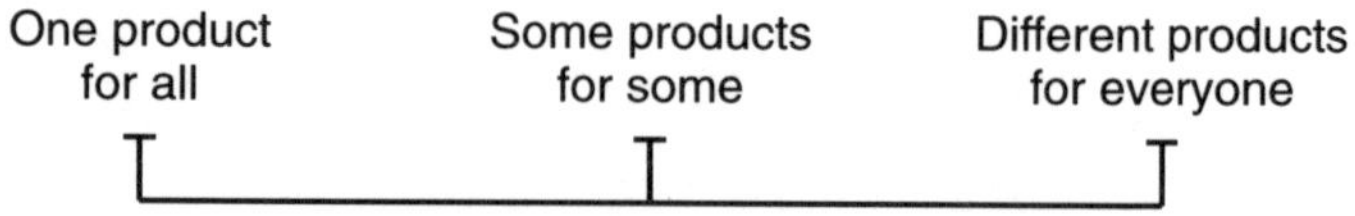

needs. Offering one product for all segments means the needs of some users are not wholly satisfied, and is therefore wasteful on resources. Taken to extremes of course, every user is a unique market segment, for everyone has slightly different needs. However, few companies have the resources to be all things to all people, and this implies that a choice needs to be made concerning which segments to serve, thus taking up a position somewhere between the two extremes in Figure 0.1.

Market segmentation also provides the key to improving a company's competitive position. Offering one product for all, that is the same or similar to competitors', is likely to cause a downward pressure on margins and a situation where only the lowest cost producer can win. Thus it makes sense to choose the segments of the market that provide the best fit with the strengths of the business. By doing so, a business will build on its specialist knowledge and expertise, enabling it to develop competitive advantage and help avoid a price attack.

Marketing, therefore, is more accurately concerned with matching organisational resources to user groupings, and this is where market segmentation can help. Consider the example shown in Figure 0.2(a). Here the market for marketing training is shown as having clusters of users, with each cluster having different needs. Within each cluster, further slight variations on these needs are represented by different, but similar, shapes.

One option for the supplier of marketing training, is to provide a general product that offers something for everybody, as shown in Figure 0.2(b). The problem with just one product is that you are really only satisfying a single group – those (represented by the circles) who want a general course. Other groups will buy if there is nothing else on offer, but they will not be fully satisfied, and they will not be prepared to pay a premium price. More crucially, they will always be looking for something better.

An alternative option would be to offer a different product for

Figure 0.2 The market for marketing training

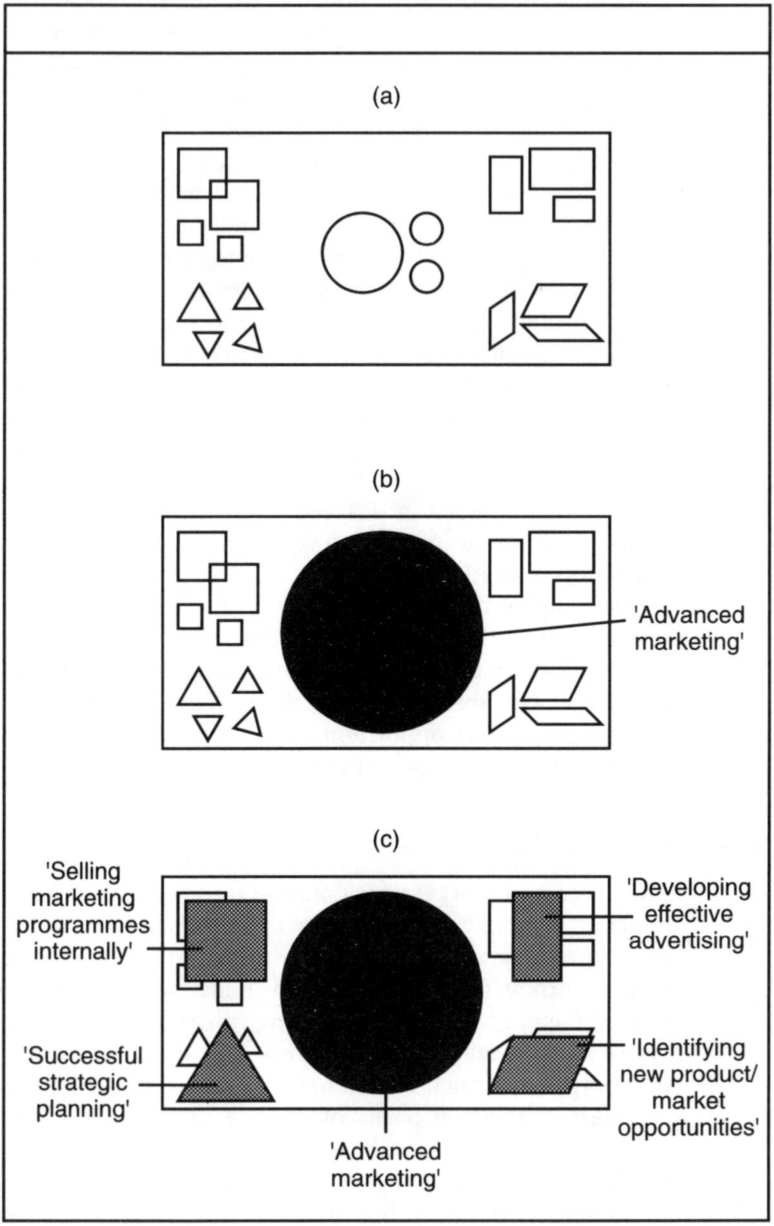

some or all of the main clusters, for example, to segment by training need, as shown in Figure 0.2(c). Now users will be happier because they are getting a product that is much closer to their needs; they will normally be prepared to pay a higher price because of that, and they will be less inclined to look elsewhere. As a supplier of marketing training, you will no doubt find that your knowledge and expertise are more suited to some segments rather than others. By targeting these areas of business strength you can look forward to not only a happier and more profitable customer base, but also one that is more secure against competitive threat.

This process of breaking up the market can continue indefinitely, and in Figure 0.2(c) may lead to segment members with a need for advertising knowledge being further sub-divided and targeted with courses for industrial advertising, consumer advertising and trade advertising. Similarly, the microsegment for industrial advertising could be divided still further, to reflect differences in 'who' has the need for knowledge. For example there will be variations in need in different industries and types of organisations, in different job functions, in different levels of experience, and so on – all of which are potential new business opportunities for the supplier of marketing training. Eventually, the point will be reached where it is no longer viable to offer a separate product or communication approach. However, and well before the point where cost becomes a concern, the business will have identified a number of product opportunities that will bring higher total sales, and a higher level of customer satisfaction for each.

WHAT ARE THE BENEFITS?

The process of market segmentation thus brings a much increased understanding of users' needs, their decision criteria and approach, and therefore gives a much clearer direction to the management of current products. This increased understanding also brings a clearer focus and return on pricing, distribution, and advertising decisions. For example, in Figure 0.2(c) the business can discard the shotgun approach it used to promote advanced marketing, and can start to think in terms of using a rifle bullet, to target each segment with a specific message about a specific product. Another notable example of a shotgun approach, concerns a well-known environmentalist group that found it was losing 60 per cent of its subscription members each year. Research with lapsed members highlighted their dissatisfaction at receiving multi-subject mailings, as well as a perceived lack of focus on their own area of interest – be it wildlife, pollution, dolphins, or whatever.

The segmentation approach also brings benefits to the search for new business growth. As it is only by selling something to someone that a business can grow, there are four possible broad courses of action as noted by Ansoff (1957) and shown in Figure 0.3. With present products, the process of segmentation can prove invaluable in identifying new market opportunities. With present markets, the insight gained into different user needs can have considerable benefit in shaping the profile against which new products are developed. Similarly, with new markets, identifying segmentation possibilities that surpass the need satisfaction attained by incumbents, will make for a more profitable entry.

However, it is in the area of selling existing products to existing markets that segmentation can often have the biggest effect. All too often businesses treat their customers as a faceless aggregation, and therefore lose out on sales opportunities with the technologies they currently have, in terms of further penetrating existing markets. With slight changes to product and/or presentation though, it is very often possible to benefit from a dramatic effect on customer satisfaction, and therefore increase both market share and profitability without moving into the more 'risky' boxes in the

Figure 0.3 Ansoff Matrix

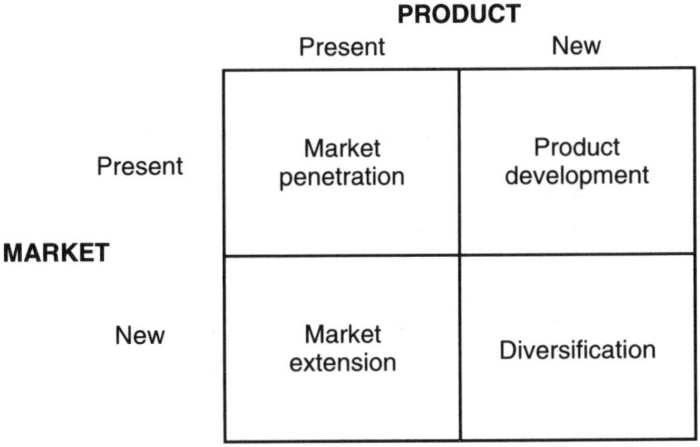

Matrix. This selling of the 'same jam in a different jar' should not be thought of as an unnecessary extra cost, nor indeed as manipulating customers. If you somehow change the presentation of a core product to give greater appeal to some user groups, and you are able to command a premium for it, then that is good business.

Unfortunately, some companies believe they are already following a segmented approach, having intuitively organised themselves around broad divisions in their customer base. However, the pursuit of a better and more efficient organisation, with its largely internal perspective, misses the point of segmentation in terms of finding better ways to meet the needs of current, and potential, customers.

Ultimately though, the biggest benefit of adopting the concept of market segmentation comes from the competitive advantage that it brings. Marketing is like playing a game, and like most games there are winners and losers. The task of marketing is to outperform the competition whilst always being mindful of the 'judge', the user, because they ultimately decide who wins. You can choose the markets you want to play in, and you can choose the products you want to play with, but the name of the game is the same: don't just be good, be better – build sustainable competitive advantage – and you will stay better.

Market segmentation thus provides a focused approach to winning the 'game', by answering the central issues facing any business, namely:

- Which groups of users should we serve?
- With whom will we compete?
- How can we outperform them?

THE MARKET SEGMENTATION PROCESS

The process of market segmentation can be broken down into a number of discrete steps as shown in Figure 0.4, and it is these steps which form the outline of the book.

In Chapter 1 we begin by defining the overall market and developing our understanding of it. In Chapter 2 we start the process of breaking down the market and identifying segments, by understanding how users differ in their purchasing approach. In Chapter 3 we begin refining and defining the emerging segments. In

Figure 0.4 The market segmentation process

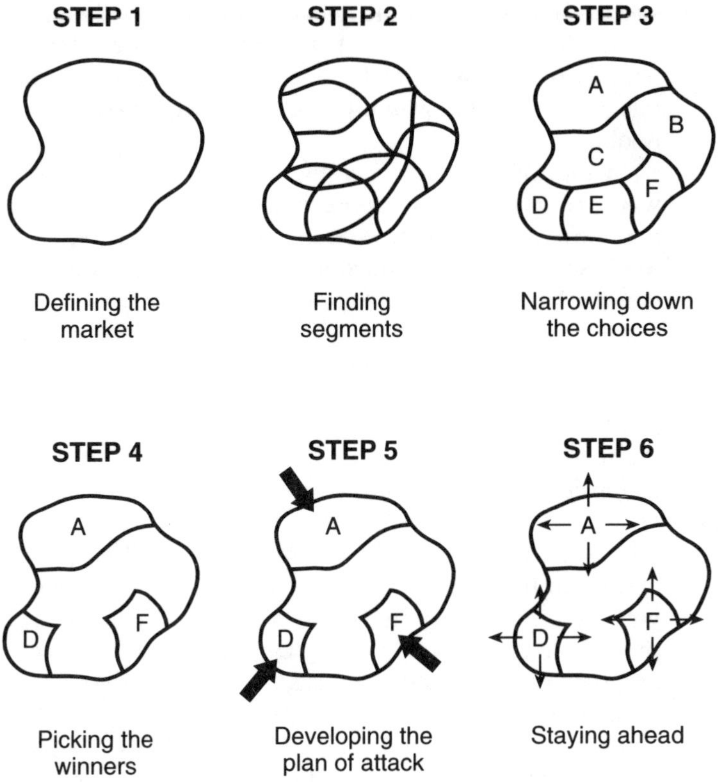

Chapter 4 we look at the techniques of evaluating and selecting the 'best' segments. In Chapter 5 we develop our plan to attack our chosen segment(s). Finally, in Chapter 6 we look at ways of staying ahead in the segment(s) we plan to enter.

MAKING THE MOST OF THE PROCESS

Before embarking on the process, and your search for new business opportunities, you should spend a few moments considering how well placed your organisation is to make the most of a technique such as market segmentation.

Success in marketing is as much to do with the way you think and act as an organisation as it is about understanding the concepts themselves. Knowledge and skills are certainly key components of success, but so too is the prevailing culture within your organisation. In short, the level of marketing orientation in your organisation is likely to be one of the biggest influences on the results you will get with a process such as the one outlined in this book.

In the following exercise there is a series of statements which will give you an early appreciation of any possible barriers that may slow your progress. You are asked to score each statement on the basis of how descriptive it is of your organisation (or one that you are familiar with) as follows:

If it is very true/always true	score 5
If it is mostly true	score 4
If it is sometimes true	score 3
If you are unsure or don't know	score 2
If it is not true/never true	score 1

Please enter your score in the space indicated by the dotted line, and try to be as accurate and as objective as you can – it will help you later in getting the most out of the market segmentation process. In fact, it would be a good idea to ask a few colleagues, in different parts of your organisation, to have a go too. When you have answered each question, add up your score for each column, and then your total score, and compare your own perceptions with those of your colleagues. An interpretation of your results is given on page 11.

EXERCISE 1 MARKETING ORIENTATION EXERCISE

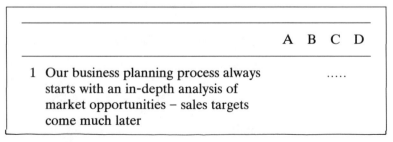

	A	B	C	D
1 Our business planning process always starts with an in-depth analysis of market opportunities – sales targets come much later			.....	

		A	B	C	D
2	Top management see marketing as an organisational orientation, and not something that individuals or departments do – at least not in isolation	.....			
3	We carry out a thorough and objective audit of our target markets at least once a year		.....		
4	Senior executives do not see themselves as operating beyond the confines of the marketing plan	.....			
5	Wherever possible we try to structure organisational activities around customer groups, rather than around functions				.....
6	Our marketing strategies are based around what will increase our competitive advantage and add value to the user, and not on vague hopes of doing better			.....	
7	Our communication programmes focus on user benefits, rather than product features				.....
8	Top management recognise that the overall goal of the organisation is about balancing customer satisfaction with making a profit	.....			
9	We always make sure market research is adequately budgeted for		.....		
10	Our marketing plan is widely used and well thumbed				.....
11	Our strategic focus is very much based on our real customer – the final consumer			.....	

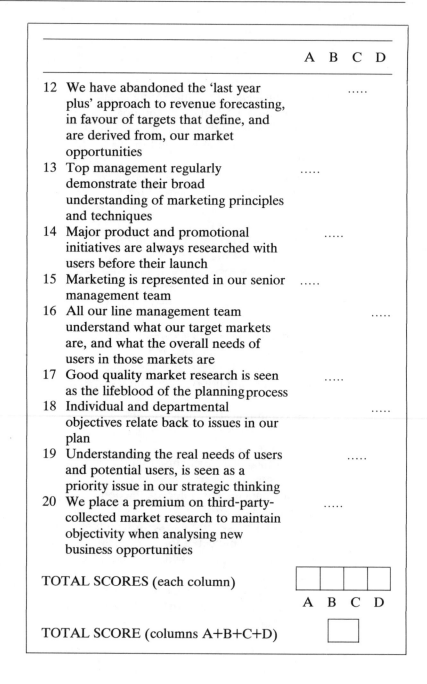

		A	B	C	D
12	We have abandoned the 'last year plus' approach to revenue forecasting, in favour of targets that define, and are derived from, our market opportunities			.....	
13	Top management regularly demonstrate their broad understanding of marketing principles and techniques	.....			
14	Major product and promotional initiatives are always researched with users before their launch		.....		
15	Marketing is represented in our senior management team	.....			
16	All our line management team understand what our target markets are, and what the overall needs of users in those markets are				.....
17	Good quality market research is seen as the lifeblood of the planning process		.....		
18	Individual and departmental objectives relate back to issues in our plan				.....
19	Understanding the real needs of users and potential users, is seen as a priority issue in our strategic thinking			.....	
20	We place a premium on third-party-collected market research to maintain objectivity when analysing new business opportunities		.....		

	A	B	C	D
TOTAL SCORES (each column)				

TOTAL SCORE (columns A+B+C+D)	

SOLUTION TO MARKETING ORIENTATION EXERCISE

The successful use of the process of market segmentation, can suffer for a number of reasons. Some of the key cultural and procedural barriers are:

a) A lack of top management commitment to/understanding of marketing. This is important, because even the best thought out plans and ideas tend to falter without the active support of senior management.
b) A lack of appreciation of the need for good quality objective information on market trends and user needs, as a basis for choosing between alternative marketing strategies; and/or a lack of resources (in terms of time, money etc.) to research target markets effectively. Information is the lifeblood of successful marketing organisations, and good information is well worth paying for.
c) The strategic focus of the organisation is not market led. It is important to look at the market first – to users and their needs, and to competitors – and *then* to develop objectives, strategies and tactical programmes, and never the other way around.
d) The correct strategic focus, when it is there, is not translated into programmes and organisational practices; and it is not communicated enough, and/or understood well enough, throughout the organisation.

In fact, the columns A–D in the exercise on pages 8–10, represent the barriers listed above. Areas of concern are indicated by any column where you scored less than 10 in total, and any individual statement where you scored 2 or less. In many cases, organisations find that their total column scores descend in value from A to D. This pattern reflects the need to address each of the potential barriers in turn: if the top management commitment is not there, good market information is unlikely to be; if the information is not there, the correct strategic focus is unlikely to be, and so on.

As each of the four columns can earn a maximum of 25 points, you will also be able to calculate your organisation's overall marketing orientation score out of 100.

If you scored less than 60, there will clearly be many areas of organisational thinking and practice that need addressing before you can get the full benefit from the process of market segmentation. Indeed, you would be well advised to consider a general marketing training course for key personnel in the organisation, to bring the overall level of marketing orientation up to a point where they can take fuller advantage of the process.

If you scored between 60–79, there will still be some areas that need addressing. An overall score of this level though, will not prevent your organisation from gaining benefit from the market segmentation process, and you will find further helpful guidance as you work through the different steps.

If you scored 80 or more, your organisation is well placed to take full and speedy advantage of the process of market segmentation.

1 *Where to begin*

This chapter focuses on the all important first step in the market segmentation process, that of defining the market. The step is important because it not only defines the scope (and length) of the segmentation exercise, but also the boundaries within which you wish to explore new business opportunities. The chapter also looks at some of the key ways of developing your understanding of the defined market, which is a necessary prerequisite to the next step, that of identifying segments.

DEFINING THE MARKET

The process of market segmentation therefore, begins with a definition of the market under consideration. There are two important aspects to defining the market:

- Needs not products
- End users not customers

It is important to phrase the market definition in terms of the overall need that is to be satisfied, and not the product that is being currently supplied. In Table 1.1 we can see some example products, together with the wider needs that they are designed to satisfy. Clearly, beginning the process with what is currently on offer is likely to channel thought processes towards current alternatives and therefore to hinder the identification of radically new products. The purpose of market segmentation is to find better ways of satisfying user needs, and of course at this stage in the process you do not know how many, or which types of products will emerge.

Table 1.1 Needs versus products

Product	*Need*	*Current alternatives*
Pills	Pain relief	Injections
Adhesives	Fastening	Screws, tape, string
Insurance	Risk protection	Savings accounts
Hamburgers	Fast food	Microwave food
Radiators	Warmth	Clothing, gas fires
Cash dispensers	Convenience	Direct debit cards
Gaskets	Leak-free joint	Jointing pastes
Car alarms	Peace of mind	Engine immobilisers

Furthermore, all products have a limited life and thus inevitably, with changing tastes and technological improvements, they come and go. Charles Revlon once remarked, 'in the factory we manufacture cosmetics, in the drug store we sell hope'. Thus cosmetics are, like any product, a means to an end, and will survive only as long as they are perceived to be the 'best' way to satisfy a given need.

It is also important here, not to confuse 'wants' with 'needs'. What users want today (for example, a hamburger), they tend not to want tomorrow (when they have for example, a pizza), but what remains unchanged is the need (in this case, for fast food). The confusion arises because users can more readily vocalize their wants, and usually it is products they are referring to. Of course, in many consumer markets it is possible to make a lot of money from satisfying wants, but they do tend to be more fickle and more short term, and invariably have to be created (often expensively) in the minds of the user. Thus, by focusing on needs, rather than wants or products, you are more likely to keep in step with market changes, and more likely to identify really new and lasting opportunities.

Similarly, it is important to clarify *whose* needs you are concerned with. Throughout this book, I have tried to avoid using the word 'customer'. Your customer is obviously someone who buys directly from you, but if they happen to be a distributor, it is important to remember that they do not drive the demand for your product – they help you supply it. As such, in many markets, it is wrong to make the 'customer' the sole focus of your strategic direction.

In consumer markets, the end user is usually very clear, but this is not always so in industrial markets. Consider the simplified example in Figure 1.1. Here, the final user is quite remote from those early on in the chain, and thus it is necessary to consider the needs of all those who subsequently add value. Nevertheless, the market needs that industrial marketers are attempting to satisfy must also, in the final analysis, be defined in terms of the requirements of the ultimate user. For example, a component manufacturer for a car engine will have to give some thought to the needs of the eventual car buyer. This wider focus will give a greater understanding of the needs of the car manufacturer (in terms of safety, noise levels and so on), who in turn must be considered for their own needs (automatic assembly, safety at work, etc.).

Figure 1.1 Know your *real* customer

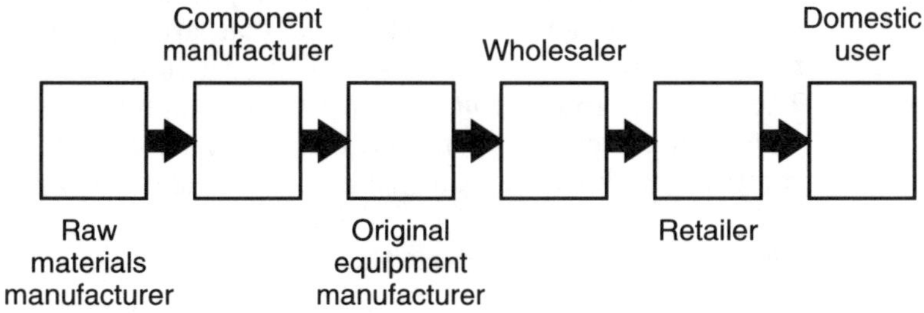

Having focused on the 'real' user and their needs, some final thought is required to develop your market definition. Often there is confusion over whether the market is to be defined in terms of the total available (i.e. all fastening methods), the potential available (i.e. all adhesive types), or the realisable available (i.e. those types of adhesives the organisation supplies). The answer to this dilemma is that it is a question of management judgment, for the process of market segmentation can occur from any point on your Market Map (see Figures 1.2 and 2.1). For those companies following a structured marketing planning process (see pages 51–5), this question is usually addressed as part of the Mission Statement.

Clearly though, market segmentation is likely to be most productive in terms of new opportunities when the market definition is kept fairly broad. However, and particularly when using the concept for the first time, it is a good idea to add some small qualification to the overall need. For example, rather than attempting to segment the market for 'entertainment', a more manageable exercise would be to tackle 'home entertainment', or even 'adult home entertainment'. Similarly, prefixing your definition with 'The UK market for ... ' or 'The industrial market for ...', will also make for a much clearer focus and one that brings earlier results.

An accurate market definition is therefore important in terms of identifying target users and their overall needs. A good definition also helps to identify relevant competitors and to calculate market shares, both of which will be important in subsequent stages of the segmentation process. Thus it is recommended that you construct a preliminary Market Map to help you to clarify your definition. In Figure 1.2, you can see an example Map that demonstrates both the variety of levels and channels that are possible in many markets, as well as indicating who the key user groups actually are. The best way to build up a Map of your market is to begin with your own current position, and then to add those of all relevant competitors. Again, it is a matter of judgment as to how widely

Figure 1.2 A simplified Market Map

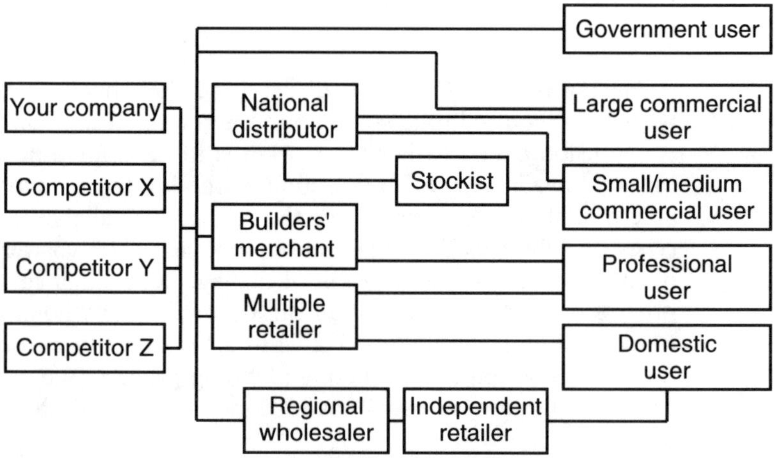

you interpret 'relevant' in defining your market, but to get the best out of the segmentation process, it should be at least some comfortable level beyond direct competitors. We will return to Market Maps in Chapter 2.

UNDERSTANDING THE MARKET

Once you have defined your market, it is very important to develop a comprehensive understanding of it before proceeding to the next step in the segmentation process. Specifically, it is important to carry out a Market Audit.

A Market Audit is a fundamental appraisal of the market and your position in it, and should form an integral part of your overall marketing planning process (see also pages 51–5). In Figure 1.3 we can see in detail what the Audit involves – the emphasis should be on collecting information, and lots of it. Much of the list will be second nature, some elements may require a bit of digging, others will require market research. However, it is difficult to imagine exploring even an existing market, without good objective information of this kind.

The Environmental Analysis concerns trends that are happening outside the market, but which may well have effects inside the market. Environmental trends could be opportunities or they could be life-threatening issues; either way, it is obviously important at least to consider them for each of the subheadings in Figure 1.3. Information on competitors is crucial, and a lot of what is required can be obtained from desk research and market intelligence. The Market Analysis is the area that will benefit the most from market research and, properly done, will provide a rich vein of new ideas to consider for future strategy. Information for the internal Company Analysis is usually the closest to hand, even if current information systems do not quite give it in precisely this format.

Most businesses do a Market Audit of sorts, the biggest crimes are either not having enough objective research, and/or simply not allowing enough time to complete it. When either crime is committed, the resulting plans tend just to reinforce current thinking and the business ploughs merrily along as before. It is also worth noting that no decisions are required in the Audit stage, because to do so very often precludes consideration of other

Figure 1.3 A Market Audit checklist

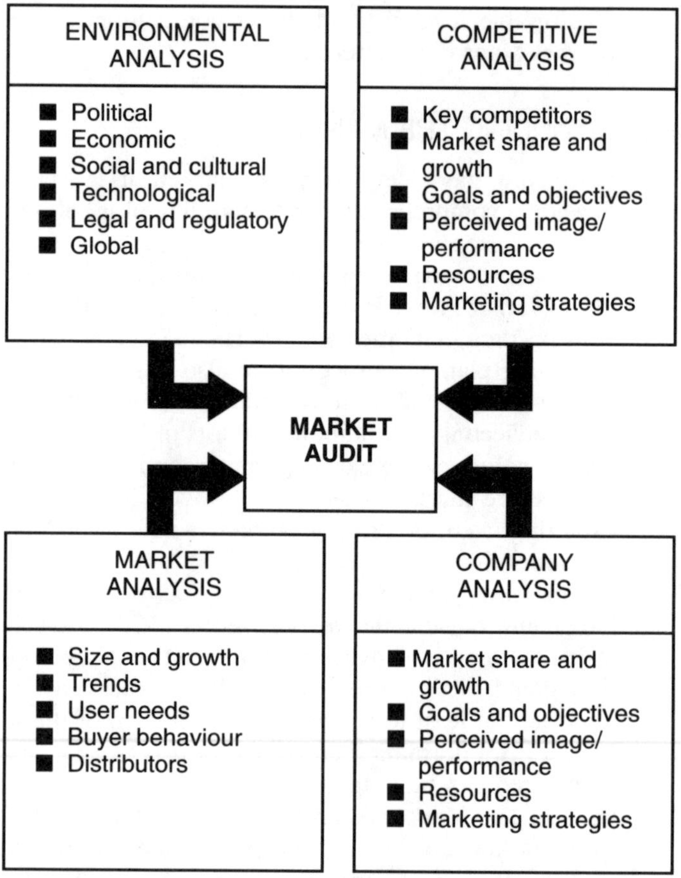

possible areas – in other words, you should stay in 'collection and analysis' mode only.

Whilst it is beyond the scope of this book to cover in detail what is required to complete an effective Market Audit, the quality and thoroughness of the analysis is an important prerequisite to successful market segmentation. McDonald and Leppard (1991) provide a more detailed methodology, but a good starting point is to break out all the subheadings in Figure 1.3, through a series of questions, and to look for trends. A summary of your current position in the market, together with details of any key trends that are likely to affect future performance, should then be written up in a concise Market Overview. Specifically, it is important to the successful use of the segmentation concept to at least have answers at the outset (and in your Overview) to the following:

- What is the total market size – actual rather than potential – and what is your market share?
- How does the market break down – by product? by user group? by distribution channel?
- What do different users *really* buy, and why? i.e. what are their needs?
- How will these needs change, say over the next 5 years?
- What benefits do you/can you offer, and what are/could be your differential benefits versus other suppliers?
- What are competitors' current/likely future strategies?
- What are the key external market trends that are likely to impact future demand?

SUMMARY OF CHAPTER 1

KEY ACTIONS	POINTS TO CONSIDER	REFERENCE
■ **Draw a Market Map to illustrate the different levels and channels, and the key user groups.**	■ **What is the current flow of goods and services from your company, or one that you are familiar with?**	■ **Figure 1.2**
■ **Choose the point on your Market Map from which you wish to begin the process of segmentation, and define the market.**	■ **What should be the scope of your search for new opportunities, in terms of the total, potential or realisable market? Remember, needs not products, end users not customers.**	■ **pp. 13–17**
■ **Write up the current market position, and any key trends, in a concise Market Overview.**	■ **What is the market size and your share of it? How are users' needs changing? What are competitors doing? What are the relevant trends in the business environment?**	■ **Figure 1.3**

2 *Finding segments*

Having defined your market and completed your Audit, you can now focus on the second step in the segmentation process, that of dividing the market into distinct groups of users who might require a different product and/or communication approach. This second step is very important to the success of the segmentation approach. Since subsequent steps focus more on evaluating and choosing between segments, a successful final result is dependent on a large amount of creative input in this one.

EXPLORING DIFFERENCES BETWEEN USERS

There are two basic approaches to dividing up a market:

- User behaviour
- User characteristics

In your Market Audit you will have collected a wealth of information on user behaviour and the more the better, since if you can explain their behaviour you are surely in a better position to sell to them. Behaviour has two aspects: first, the more tangible things that are bought; second, why users behave the way they do.

There are several theories of why users behave the way they do. One theory refers to the rational buyer, whose principal concerns are price, quality and delivery. Another view seeks to explain behaviour via attitudes, perceptions, aspirations, and so on. Yet another explains behaviour in terms of benefits sought by users when they buy a product.

Similarly, in your Market Audit, you will have noted differences in attributes, or characteristics, between user types. This too is important, since having found behavioural differences between users, you then need to be able to describe the user groups so that you can address them with your new product and/or promotional programmes.

Thus the process of breaking down the market is best done by brainstorming differences between users, and asking:

- Who buys? (user characteristics)
- What do they buy? } (user behaviour)
- Why do they buy? }

By continually asking these three questions you can open up many different possible bases for segmenting the market in question, as shown in Table 2.1 (p. 25). It is often helpful when brainstorming a current market, to begin with 'who buys' and to expand the preliminary Market Map you developed in Chapter 1 (see Figure 1.2). Using your market definition, you should redraw your Market Map from the point at which segmentation is to occur, and then add to it all the variations in 'who buys'. Using our earlier example in Figure 1.2, and focusing on large commercial users, an illustration of how the different buying groups might begin to break down is shown in Figure 2.1. The Map can obviously be extended further to show, for example, car manufacturers and parts manufacturers as divisions of automotive, and so on. Having expanded

Figure 2.1 An expanded Market Map

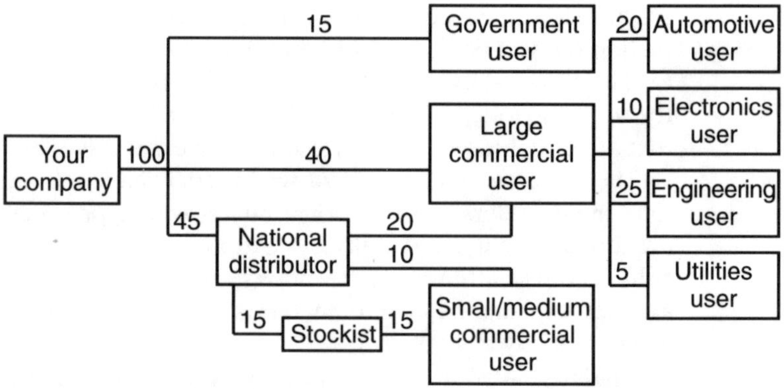

your Market Map along these lines, you can then indicate how 100 units of your own and each of your competitors' products find their way to the different user groups, and thus establish 'who buys what'.

The next stage is to brainstorm 'why do they buy', i.e. what is the user group trying to achieve with their purchase. Clearly, it is important that your analysis of why things are bought should be undertaken from the perspective of the user, and not, for example, solely on the basis of product features or technology. Users go into the market looking for a particular bundle of benefits – if you go offering product features, you run the risk of not meeting up with them. Thus it is important to consider those elements of the

Figure 2.2 The importance of the Product Surround

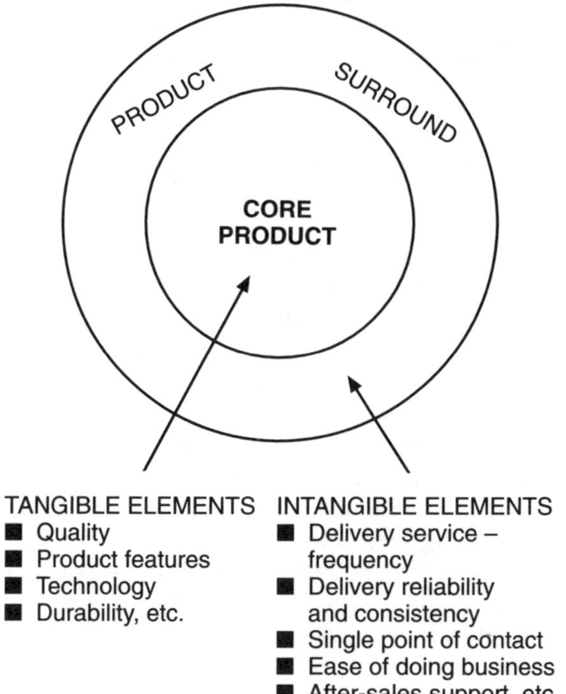

Source: Christopher (1992)

product 'surround' as shown in Figure 2.2, not least because they often account for as much as 80 per cent of the impact of the final product offering, for only as little as 20 per cent of the costs.

Some of the ideas that are generated in your brainstorming will be more relevant than others but, at this stage, it is important to record them all. Equally, some of the ideas you will recognise and may indeed be acknowledging in your current marketing programmes, but recording these too is a necessary step to bringing out others, so as to develop a comprehensive understanding of user differences. It is also advisable, for the time being, to keep to broad segmentation bases only as illustrated in Table 2.1. Clearly it makes for a more manageable exercise to identify the broad bases first, before subsequently screening them (see pages 35–7), and then breaking out all their finer variations (see pages 37–40). Focusing on these user differences first, as a separate step, also increases your chances of finding new and different ways to approach the market. A fuller list of possible segmentation bases and their variables, is included in the Appendix.

SEGMENTING IN DIFFERENT MARKETS

A Consumer markets

Although market segmentation has proved a difficult concept to turn into reality, it is normally considered to be easier in consumer markets. In most consumer markets the quality of information and the opportunities for mass communication make for a speedier segmentation process and quicker results. The biggest difficulty in segmenting consumer markets is coming to grips with the 'inner mind' of the user. Some of the more common bases used in consumer markets are shown in Table 2.1.

Demographic differences have been widely used as bases for segmenting consumer markets. For example, 'age' is used as a basis for charging different prices in the travel market and, in other markets, quite different products are targeted at the slightest of differences in age groups – typically many baby products. Similarly, 'family size' is used as a segmentation base for products such as fridges, and 'sex' is used as a segmentation base for products such as maternity clothing, as well as products used by both sexes, such as golf clubs. Increasingly, products like cars,

Table 2.1 Segmentation bases for consumer markets

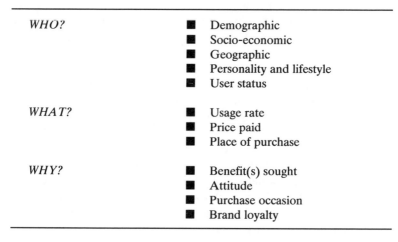

WHO?	■ Demographic ■ Socio-economic ■ Geographic ■ Personality and lifestyle ■ User status
WHAT?	■ Usage rate ■ Price paid ■ Place of purchase
WHY?	■ Benefit(s) sought ■ Attitude ■ Purchase occasion ■ Brand loyalty

hand tools and adhesives are being targeted at females, to stimulate wider usage and to reflect their influence on purchasing decisions.

It should be noted though, that demographic bases alone, rarely provide a complete understanding of user differences, i.e. users within the same demographic group will not always share the same buying behaviour and usage patterns. For example, the 'young at heart' or the 'mature beyond their years', are unlikely to conform to the behavioural norm for their actual age groups.

Socio-economic differences such as 'income' and 'social class', are also important in understanding spending and usage patterns in many consumer markets. As income rises, consumers typically seek better housing, better food and wider recreational activities. Similarly, social class can be a strong influence on preferences in clothing, education, reading habits and leisure activities. Some organisations, such as banks, combine social class differences with key demographic differences such as life stage. By comparing market penetration against the population for each social class/life stage group, the bank aims to identify unserved areas and thus possible new business opportunities. The effect of socio-economic differences though, can be distorted by within-group variations such as those in personal tastes, ambitions and social trends. For example, a dual income family is very likely to have different purchasing patterns to other families in their traditional socio-economic grouping.

Geographic differences are probably the oldest bases used for market segmentation. Traditionally some food, clothing and heating markets were segmented in this way, but to some extent these differences have been blurred by the growth of multiple retail organisations, and consequently the wider availability and standardisation of many of the products. The beer market for example, is gradually losing many of its regional product variations.

In most of today's consumer markets, demographic, geographic and socio-economic differences are tending to become rather superficial methods of grouping users. As we have seen, these more traditional bases rarely go far enough in terms of explaining buyer behaviour to marketers. For example, there will be a big difference in product offer and promotional message between the demographically young and the psychologically young. Furthermore, in mature markets these first stage differences will be well catered for, and analysis of them is less likely to uncover unsatisfied needs.

There is, of course, a wealth of available information on these traditional bases and their variables, and this is important to marketers. If your chosen segments reflect behavioural or psychological differences between users, it will still be important to understand, for example, their demographic characteristics, so that you can measure the size of the segment and target it efficiently (see Table 5.4, page 63).

Personality and attitude differences often make it worthwhile to offer different products, use different prices, and/or distribute products differently. These psychological differences can be identified through consumer surveys, and they can be a powerful segmentation base when brand propositions are developed to match them. The increasing awareness of environmental concerns is a good example of an attitude that can be the dominant purchasing criteria. Similarly, some individuals are positively disposed to new ideas, and because of this personality trait are more likely to adopt new products. Robertson (1971) has noted that those who adopt new products early tend to have higher income, are better educated, are younger, read more, and will use more of the product concerned. Although it is sometimes difficult to detect a generalised pattern of behaviour arising from psycho-

Table 2.2 Benefit segments in the less expensive camera market

The 'do-it-yourselfer' (25%)	*The 'black box user' (40%)*	*The 'timid photographer' (35%)*
Great pride in good pictures	Taking pictures considered a necessary evil	Great pride in good pictures
Gratification from making settings and adjustments	Little pride expressed if the picture is good	High perceived risk that pictures will not be good
Pride in a complex camera	Desire for camera to be as simple as possible	No confidence in ability to manipulate camera and settings
Regards a good picture the result of his expertise		Desires camera to guarantee a good picture without his effort

Source: Engle, Fiorello and Cayley (1972)

logical differences, it is always advisable to analyse consumer markets to check for them.

There are also a number of behavioural bases for segmentation that can be used to explain differences between users, and very often these are the most productive in terms of identifying new business opportunities.

User status, usage rate and *brand loyalty* are examples of commonly used behavioural bases. Markets can be segmented into non-users, potential users, ex-users, first time users and regular users. Regular users can be further divided into light, medium and heavy users. Similarly, users of all types can be divided into those that are loyal, and those that are not.

Obviously it makes sense to target heavy users, where the return on the marketing pound will be much greater. Heavy users, for example of beer, also tend to have common demographic characteristics and media habits, which helps in the development of the product offer and promotional message. Potential users and non-loyal users are also worthy of marketing effort, though obviously of a different type, and ex-users are worthy of further analysis if only to learn of marketing weaknesses.

Benefits perceived by users for a product or service can be a particularly powerful segmentation base. Haley (1968) found four benefit segments in the toothpaste market (see Table 5.4, page 63), and Yankelovich (1964) found three benefit segments in the market for wrist-watches – two of which were not being exploited by the leading watch companies at that time. Engle, Fiorello and Cayley (1972) illustrate in Table 2.2, how this approach can lead to the identification of different product opportunities and promotional messages. Benefits sought can include quality, performance, image, service and so on, and these are very often the most insightful of segmentation bases simply because they deal directly with user needs.

Purchase occasions can also be used to explain how users approach purchase decisions, and subsequent marketing effort can focus attention on increasing these occasions, or exploiting others where the same purchasing criteria is likely to apply. For example, some financial services companies have developed products for key life stage occasions such as critical illness, and income protection during short-term illness or following redundancy.

Thus it is recommended that the focus of your attention in this

Table 2.3 Segmentation bases and consumer products

Segmentation base	*Typical products*
Age	Insurance, baby products, toys, travel
Attitude	Environmentally friendly products
Benefit sought	Toothpaste, wrist-watches, cameras
Brand loyalty	Grocery products, cigarettes, toiletries
Family size	Consumer durables, e.g. fridges
Geographic	Petrol, water softeners
Income	Housing, household furnishings
Lifestyle	Alcoholic drinks, cars, 24-hour banking
Personality	Clothing, high-tech products
Purchase occasion	Confectionery, greeting cards, air travel
Religion	Food types, gift purchases
Sex	Bicycles, golf clubs, hairdressing
Social class	Antiques, private education, newspapers
Usage rate	Beer, paint

second step of the process be on understanding the behavioural differences between users. Nevertheless, it pays in terms of developing a fuller understanding of all user differences to follow through the who, what and why approach, beginning with your Market Map. There will be a temptation to jump around in your brainstorming session and to focus on what might seem the more productive bases, and to a degree this should be encouraged. The overriding consideration though, must be to consider *all* possible user differences.

Some further examples of segmentation bases, that have been used with different consumer products, are shown in Table 2.3.

B Industrial markets

In industrial markets, segmentation can appear to be more difficult, not least because the organisation is often quite remote from the final user, as we saw in Figure 1.1. Also, industrial products sometimes have multiple applications, and indeed several different products can be used for the same application. Similarly, industrial users differ greatly and themselves operate in vastly diverse markets and, as such, it is not always easy to determine what is key for strategy. Certainly there are fewer published sources of industrial market information, which can be a constraint where a large number of unfamiliar segments need to be evaluated.

All too often though, industrial companies assume they are 'doing it already' when it comes to segmenting their market or, worse still, deliberately ignore it believing it to be too difficult. The difficulties often arise from a lack of a marketing orientation and a belief that new business ideas only ever come from the inside, or from customer requests. Sometimes industrial companies unknowingly segment their activities, but they lack a disciplined approach to understanding who buys what and why, and fail to exploit it on any significant scale. At other times segmentation is used, but only to assess past product performance, rather than to develop effective marketing programmes.

However, this second step of dividing up the market, and the subsequent analysis of segments, should follow the same basic methodology irrespective of market type. The choice of segmentation bases in industrial markets is clearly key, and certainly they are of a different type to consumer markets, as can be seen in Table 2.4.

Organisational differences such as industry type and company size, are usually the easiest to identify with information being readily available via government statistics, trade sources, industry directories, and so on. For companies selling to a wide variety of industries, or having restricted capacity and resources, these can be productive bases for segmentation, but recognising such differences is often less useful than understanding why organisations buy. As we noted earlier (see page 26), organisational (or demographic) differences rarely go far enough in terms of explaining purchasing decisions, and thus their exclusive use fails to explore the full potential of the market segmentation approach.

Operating differences such as companies that use a relevant manufacturing process or a related product, or that use the product for a particular end-use application, can often prove attractive bases for targeting new customers. Similarly, identifying the various categories of user status and usage rate can, as we noted in consumer markets, be advantageous when responded to with different marketing programmes. Operating differences tend to be quite stable, and therefore make for lasting segments, and segment members can very often be identified from internal sources of information.

Table 2.4 Segmentation bases for industrial markets

WHO?	■ Industry type ■ Size of company ■ Geographic location ■ Technological base ■ User status
WHAT?	■ End-use application ■ Volume used ■ Price paid ■ Product specification
WHY?	■ Purchasing policy ■ Buyer/seller relationship ■ Buyer personality ■ Benefit(s) sought

Behavioural differences are often the most enlightening when it comes to understanding purchasing approach and criteria, although they tend to be less stable, and usually require bespoke user research to identify them. Differences in buyer behaviour can be accounted for by company purchasing policy: some companies seek particular types of suppliers, others just one supplier; some decide to buy in a particular way, for example, through a tender; some want to pay in a particular way, for example, through leasing. Similarly, the behaviour of key individuals in the buying organisation – in terms of their motivations, perceptions, and so on – can represent crucial behavioural differences and therefore possible bases. Perhaps the most powerful behavioural base for segmenting industrial markets is according to benefits sought, i.e. by grouping users on the basis of their similarity of needs. In many of today's industrial markets, commercial success has moved beyond simply targeting different industries and applications, as users look for an additional mix of quality, image, technical service, parts availability, and so on, in addition to a basic product performance.

Thus it is recommended that you approach your search for segmentation bases in industrial markets in a similar manner to that which we have discussed for consumer markets. Wind and Cardoza (1974) suggest the 'who, what and why' approach can be grouped into two stages. The first stage involves identifying macro-segments through such bases as (a) end-use market, (b) product application, (c) usage rate, (d) customer size, and (e) geographic location. The second stage involves sub-dividing the macro-segments into microsegments, using bases such as (a) job position, (b) personal characteristics, (c) perceived product importance, (d) attitudes towards vendor, and (e) stage in the buying process.

Shapiro and Bonoma (1984) suggest a similar sequential approach in five stages: demographics; operating variables; purchasing approach; situational factors, such as delivery urgency, product end use and order size; and the personal characteristics of buyers. As you move through the five stages, they argue, the differences become less visible and less permanent, but require more intimate knowledge, and thus you are more likely to uncover unserved needs.

To allow you to make a start in brainstorming industrial markets, some of the more commonly used segmentation bases are summarised in Table 2.4.

C International markets

The many advantages of market segmentation techniques in domestic markets are equally applicable in an international setting. The key aspect of international market segmentation, as with industrial markets, is choosing the right bases, since international markets can be divided up in an almost infinite number of ways.

Inevitably geographic, socio-economic and political bases are used to establish differences between international users, and these are important – marketing textbooks are littered with examples of new products that have failed to take account of them. However, market segmentation by these environmental bases alone is unlikely to be the most productive approach (unless regions are homogeneous with respect to other marketing variables), since they do not provide an effective and sustainable barrier to competitive attack.

Wind and Douglas (1972) suggest treating the world market as one single market, and looking for groups of users which transcend national borders, but possess common characteristics relevant to the marketing activity. Baalbaki and Malhotra (1993) suggest that the traditional environmental differences should be supplemented with a second stage that involves identifying homogeneity of response to market stimuli, such as product, price, promotion or distribution initiatives.

Again though, it should be noted that the essential principles and methodology of segmentation remain the same, whatever the market. A successful outcome lies in the creativity that is applied to the segmentation process – particularly to this second step of brainstorming who buys what, and why – and not in any fundamental differences in approach.

BRAINSTORMING – SOME POINTS TO REMEMBER

- Brainstorming user differences is best conducted as part of the Audit stage of the marketing plan (see pages 17–19 and 53), so that participants can have some pre-reading on current trends in the market.
- Use cross-functional groups, of similar seniority from within the organisation, and ideally supplement with industry 'experts' from outside. Remember, segmentation is far too important to be left to the Marketing Department!
- Care should be taken with the composition of personalities within the group, so that a balanced view emerges.
- A skilled facilitator is required to maintain objectivity, and to keep a high level of motivation within the group.
- Focus on user needs, and do not be driven by what you currently offer.
- Develop your Market Map to help you in brainstorming the 'who, what and why' of user differences. Remember, quality comes out of quantity.
- Keep to broad segmentation bases only – exploring all the finer variations (the segmentation variables) at this stage, will make for an unwieldy and unfocused exercise.
- Avoid jumping ahead and thinking too early about new product solutions – it may preclude consideration of other possible variations in user needs.
- Record everything. Instant judgments on the suitability of segmentation bases will probably leave you with what you are currently working on.
- Remember that segments do not last forever – users' perceptions and needs will change.

SUMMARY OF CHAPTERS 1–2

KEY ACTIONS	POINTS TO CONSIDER	REFERENCE
■ Market Map	■ The flow of goods to the final user	■ Figure 1.2
■ Market definition	■ The scope of your search for new opportunities	■ pp. 13–17
■ Market Audit	■ The current market position and key trends	■ Figure 1.3
■ **Using your Market Map and your Audit, develop a comprehensive list of possible segmentation bases.**	■ **How do users differ in terms of their buying behaviour and characteristics, i.e. who buys, what do they buy, and why? Remember, quality comes out of quantity.**	■ **Tables 2.1, 2.3 and 2.4**

3 *Narrowing down the choices*

The third step in the market segmentation process can often begin with as many as fifty possible bases for dividing up your market. In this chapter, we begin selecting the 'best' segments by narrowing down and refining the choices.

It is of course important that the previous step be kept separate from this one – that the process of dividing up the market, be separated from the selection of attractive segments – so as not to preclude identification of other possible bases. However, it is a good idea to use the same team of people in this stage, to build ownership in your final choice and to maintain a continuity of approach.

REFINING THE SEGMENTATION BASES

Your first task is an initial screening of the list of bases developed in your brainstorming session. To be effective your final segmentation bases must be:

- Relevant
- Substantial
- Accessible

Using your list, first of all eliminate the differences between users that are just not appropriate to the market in question, i.e. those that are not relevant to the purchase situation. For example, age and sex will represent differences between users in most consumer markets, but in some they will not influence the purchase decision. Inevitably, some of the bases you have identified will not be relevant, but this should be taken as a good sign, since it means that your brainstorming stage has stayed focused on user differences and not been tempted into instant judgments.

Second, make a note against any bases that are unlikely to be large and/or profitable enough to justify specific products and/or promotions. Kotler (1976) suggests that a final segment should be the largest possible group worthy of targeting with a tailored marketing programme. You may feel comfortable eliminating some bases that are just too insubstantial, but beware of over-pruning your list. It is very often feasible, and desirable (see page 39), to combine two or more bases to create a segment that will justify a separate approach.

Then, with your remaining bases, concentrate first on those for which you are most likely to be able to effectively target segment members. Clearly, the ability to identify and reach the segment is important if you are to turn user differences to your advantage. For example, your promotional campaigns would obviously be more effective if you could target a specific user group which you knew had a favourable attitude to your product, but their media habits may not be discernible from those who do not. Similarly, if you can identify the user group, then you will more easily judge its size and purchasing power, which will help in the financial justification of any new product(s) and/or promotional message(s).

This screening approach will provide an initial judgment as to which bases are likely to be most fruitful for you to explore further. However, it is important that the unused analysis to date is not

Table 3.1 Possible segmentation bases for a domestic boiler manufacturer

	Relevant	*Substantial*	*Accessible*
User location	Yes	Yes	Yes
Years in house	No	Yes	Yes
Age of boiler	Yes	Yes	No
Age of house	Yes	Yes	Yes
Religion	No	Yes	No
Water only	Yes	No	No
Size of kitchen	Yes	Yes	Yes

lost. By screening your bases in this way, you are likely to identify user differences that will bring the biggest and quickest sales opportunities. Early success will then bring the necessary confidence in the wider process, to explore some of the more obscure, and possibly more lucrative bases, at a later date.

A simplified approach to the process of narrowing down the choices is shown in Table 3.1. Segmentation bases that are both relevant, substantial and accessible should, therefore, proceed to the next stage.

IDENTIFYING THE SEGMENTATION VARIABLES

Having narrowed down your list of segmentation bases to a more appropriate and manageable number – typically eight to ten – you can now break down and define the emerging segments.

The process of breaking down the bases involves identifying the segmentation variables, as illustrated in Figure 3.1. Using your narrowed down list of bases, and by developing a number of supplementary questions, it is possible to subdivide each base to identify quite specific user groups and needs.

The approach illustrated in Figure 3.1 is referred to as the Fishbone Technique, and was developed by Majaro (1988). The technique is a very useful way of structuring information when trying to solve a problem with multiple causes. You will have already identified the 'bones' of the answer through your analysis of possible segmentation bases, but this will only give you a superficial picture of new business opportunities. By asking 'who', 'what' or 'why' again, for each bone on the fish, you will be able to develop a much more precise understanding (i.e. the segmentation variables) of each base, in terms of user groups and their needs.

Whilst it is not essential to have the benefit of user-based research at this stage, undoubtedly the realisation will occur that in some areas you do not have complete information. However, it is sufficient to use 'best judgment' at this stage, and to make a note to check any key assumptions in the later stages. Some further examples of segmentation bases and their likely variables are shown in the Appendix.

Once the process of breaking down the bases has been exhausted, it is possible to conceptualise your market opportunities in matrix form as shown in Figure 3.2.

Figure 3.1: Identifying segmentation variables

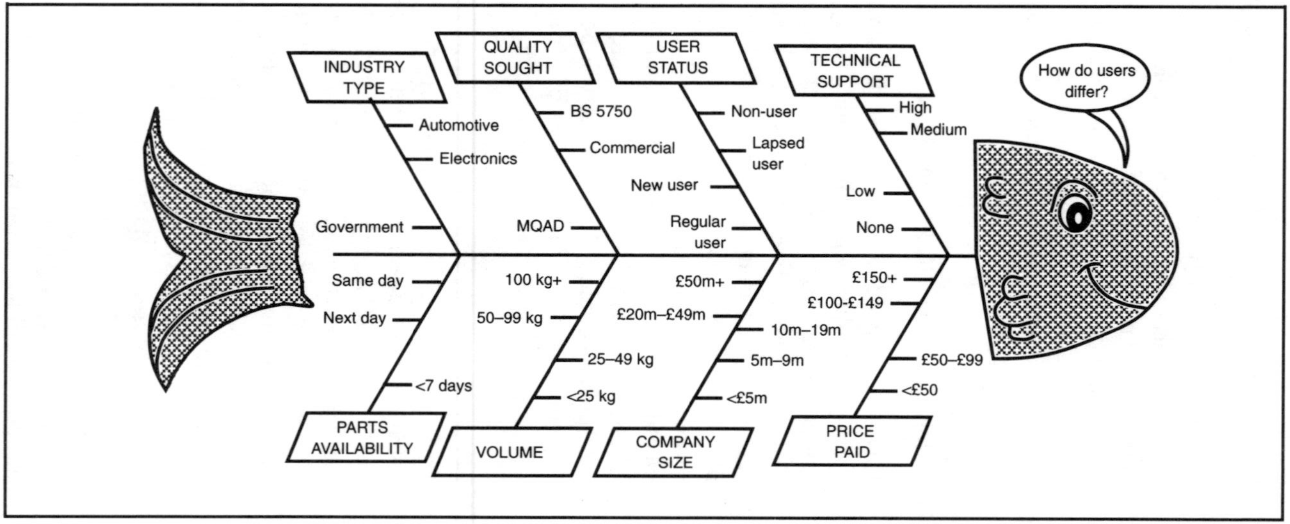

In can be seen from Figure 3.2 that, even with three bases, and four segmentation variables for each, we have identified sixty-four possible segments! Therefore at this stage, it is a good idea to re-appraise your bases/variables and group together segments with similar reasons for buying. Additionally, a final test of substantiality needs to be applied to ensure a manageable exercise that yields early results. Where possible this final screening should involve estimates of profit potential, or at least a quantifiable judgment as to whether the emerging segment is likely to be large enough to warrant a separate marketing programme.

Figure 3.2: An example Segment Matrix

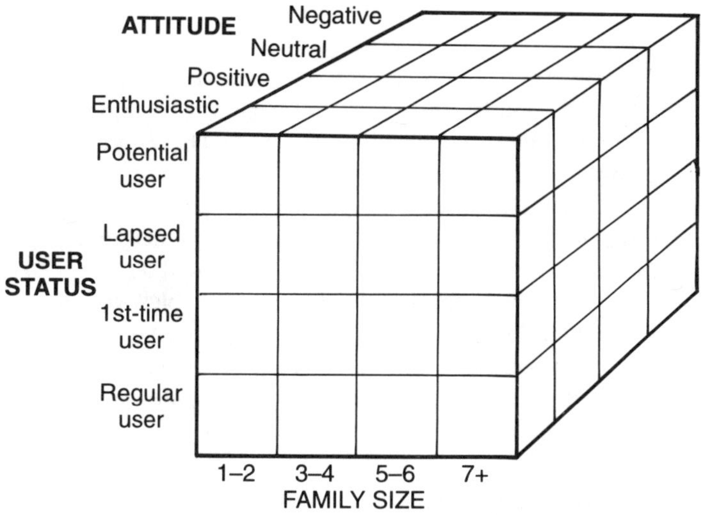

As we noted in Chapter 2, in many of today's competitive markets this type of multi-stage approach – or grouping together of segmentation bases – is vital to identifying new areas and to building a differential advantage over competitors. For example, a financial services company looking to segment the market for pensions and life assurance (need: long-term security), identified a segment made up of those who 'don't have' (segmentation base: user status), who 'would like' (base: attitude), but 'don't understand' (base: knowledge), and yet 'can afford' (base: income).

Figure 3.3: An example Segment Tree

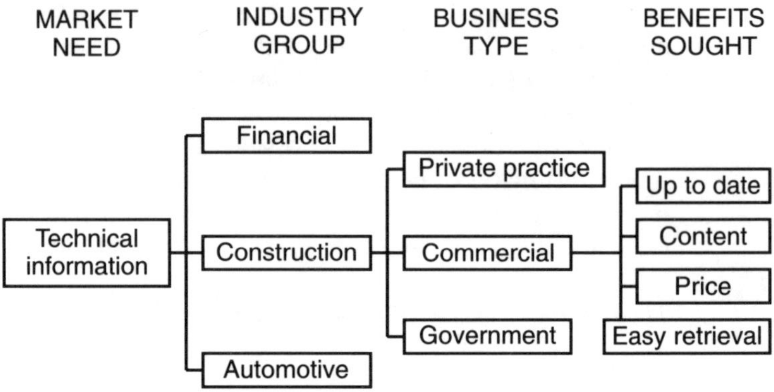

In Figure 3.3 you can see an example of a publishing company which supplies technical information, taking a multi-stage approach to segmenting its market. The Segment Tree can be completed to show all possible permutations, and providing each branch is substantial enough, the company can begin to think in terms of targeting each with a specific product and/or promotional message. Thus you should use the Segment Tree approach to help you to finally appraise the bases/ variables you have identified while completing Figure 3.1. Starting with 'who buys' (or industry type, company size and user status, from Figure 3.1), and working from left to right, you will more quickly develop a picture of the more attractive and substantial business opportunities.

DEFINING THE SEGMENT

Your final task then, at this stage, is to define each emerging segment in a sentence. Using the bases in Figure 3.2, each definition would reflect a user group of a particular family size and user status, and having a certain attitude. Using the bases in Figure 3.3, the definitions would reflect an industry/business/benefit sought combination, for example:

> Commercial users in the construction industry, who have the need for up-to-date technical information.

ecutives from a cross-section of functions having an input. greed, the same factors must obviously be used for all the ts, because determining relative attractiveness is the aim at ge.

e key segment attractiveness factors are as follows:

nt size
nt growth
of competition
nt profitability
technological changes
vity to price
s to entry
or supplier bargaining power
political considerations
lity and seasonality
cle position

sly, not all your chosen factors will be of equal importance, such it pays to adopt a simple weighting system (say, out of egment size and growth are normally desirable factors in arkets, though some organisations choose to apply a lower ng to them, either because they do not have the resources, use they fear the segment will be attractive to too many Having applied a weighting, and using a simple 0–10 system, a ranking of your shortlist of definitions can be developed.

.1 Segment attractiveness evaluation

	10	*5*	*0*	*Score*	*Weight*	*Rank*
l of competition	>20	10–19	<10	5	20	1.0
ent growth (%pa)	>10	5–9	<5	10	30	3.0
l of competition	Low	Medium	High	0	10	0.0
tability (%)	>15	10–14	<10	5	30	1.5
nological change	Low	Medium	High	5	10	0.5
			TOTAL		100	6.0

At this stage, it is also important to make a final check that members of each segment not only have a high degree of similarity in terms of their needs, i.e. they are internally homogeneous, but that they are also very different from other segments. This final qualification of 'distinctiveness' will allow you the possibility of pursuing a different, and higher overall, pricing policy for each segment. In other words, having subsequently developed different 'value packages' for different segments, you would not want a lower price to be the cause of switching. Checking for distinctiveness, is most easily done whilst completing the 'branches' of your Segment Tree.

Experience shows that the steps in Chapters 1–3 can take up to half a day or more, and that a clear result is only just becoming apparent at the end of that. However, the outcome of these first three steps should be a more comprehensive and in-depth understanding of differing user needs, together with the first signs of groups of users, or segments, where the organisation can do more or better.

SUMMARY OF CHAPTERS 1–3

KEY ACTIONS	POINTS TO CONSIDER	REFERENCE
■ Market Map	■ The flow of goods to the final user	■ Figure 1.2
■ Market definition	■ The scope of your search for new opportunities	■ pp. 13–17
■ Market Audit	■ The current market position and key trends	■ Figure 1.3
■ Brainstorming	■ Who buys, what do they buy, and why?	■ Tables 2.1, 2.3 and 2.4

■ **Refine your list of segmentation bases to those which are likely to be the most productive, in terms of new business opportunities.**	■ **Are they relevant to the purchase situation? Are they substantial enough to justify a tailored marketing programme? Are the user groups easy to identify and reach?**	■ **Table 3.1**
■ **Break out all the possible segmentation variables for your refined list.**	■ **What are the precise needs/user groups for each of your segmentation bases?**	■ **Figures 3.1 and 3.2**
■ **Draw a Segment Tree and define each emerging segment in a sentence.**	■ **Can the segmentation variables be grouped together to make more substantial and/or attractive segments. Are they distinct enough from each other?**	■ **Figure 3.3**

4 *Picking th*

In many ways, once po
defined, the more difficu
tation are over – cert
manageable, and more p
However, from here o
arguably bigger and mor
In this chapter we loo
prioritising the 'best' s
aspects to picking the wi

- Determining segment att
- Judging segment fit with
- Matching attractiveness

DETERMINING SEGMENT A

Your first task in priorit
their attractiveness to y
process, for which you d
purely an internal decisi
to the organisation.
Using your list of seg
choose the most relevan
group of segments unc
possible attractiveness f
though, to keep your fin
otherwise the exercise b
Again, the final selection

key e
Once
segme
this st
So

Segme
Segme
Level
Segme
Likely
Sensit
Barrie
Buyer
Socio-
Cyclic
Life-c

Obvic
and a
100).
most
weigh
or be
others
scorin
quick

Table

Facto

1 Lev
2 Seg
3 Lev
4 Pro
5 Tec

4 *Picking the winners*

In many ways, once possible segments have been identified and defined, the more difficult and arduous aspects of market segmentation are over – certainly by now you should have a more manageable, and more precise, list of new business opportunities. However, from here onwards, the decisions you will take are arguably bigger and more crucial.

In this chapter we look at the next step, that of identifying and prioritising the 'best' segments, and there are three important aspects to picking the winners:

- Determining segment attractiveness
- Judging segment fit with business strengths
- Matching attractiveness to strengths

DETERMINING SEGMENT ATTRACTIVENESS

Your first task in prioritising segments is to list them according to their attractiveness to you. This is a relatively straightforward process, for which you do not need user-market research, since it is purely an internal decision as to what makes a segment attractive to the organisation.

Using your list of segment definitions developed in Chapter 3, choose the most relevant criteria for judging attractiveness for the group of segments under consideration. Some suggestions for possible attractiveness factors are shown below. It is advisable though, to keep your final list to no more than five or six factors, otherwise the exercise becomes too complex and loses its focus. Again, the final selection of factors should be a team decision, with key executives from a cross-section of functions having an input. Once agreed, the same factors must obviously be used for all the segments, because determining relative attractiveness is the aim at this stage.

Some key segment attractiveness factors are as follows:

- Segment size
- Segment growth
- Level of competition
- Segment profitability
- Likely technological changes
- Sensitivity to price
- Barriers to entry
- Buyer or supplier bargaining power
- Socio-political considerations
- Cyclicality and seasonality
- Life-cycle position

Obviously, not all your chosen factors will be of equal importance, and as such it pays to adopt a simple weighting system (say, out of 100). Segment size and growth are normally desirable factors in most markets, though some organisations choose to apply a lower weighting to them, either because they do not have the resources, or because they fear the segment will be attractive to too many others. Having applied a weighting, and using a simple 0–10 scoring system, a ranking of your shortlist of definitions can be quickly developed.

Table 4.1 Segment attractiveness evaluation

Factor	*10*	*5*	*0*	*Score*	*Weight*	*Rank*
1 Level of competition	>20	10–19	<10	5	20	1.0
2 Segment growth (%pa)	>10	5–9	<5	10	30	3.0
3 Level of competition	Low	Medium	High	0	10	0.0
4 Profitability (%)	>15	10–14	<10	5	30	1.5
5 Technological change	Low	Medium	High	5	10	0.5
				TOTAL	100	6.0

■ Refine your list of segmentation bases to those which are likely to be the most productive, in terms of new business opportunities.	**■ Are they relevant to the purchase situation? Are they substantial enough to justify a tailored marketing programme? Are the user groups easy to identify and reach?**	**■ Table 3.1**
■ Break out all the possible segmentation variables for your refined list.	**■ What are the precise needs/user groups for each of your segmentation bases?**	**■ Figures 3.1 and 3.2**
■ Draw a Segment Tree and define each emerging segment in a sentence.	**■ Can the segmentation variables be grouped together to make more substantial and/or attractive segments. Are they distinct enough from each other?**	**■ Figure 3.3**

At this stage, it is also important to make a final check that members of each segment not only have a high degree of similarity in terms of their needs, i.e. they are internally homogeneous, but that they are also very different from other segments. This final qualification of 'distinctiveness' will allow you the possibility of pursuing a different, and higher overall, pricing policy for each segment. In other words, having subsequently developed different 'value packages' for different segments, you would not want a lower price to be the cause of switching. Checking for distinctiveness, is most easily done whilst completing the 'branches' of your Segment Tree.

Experience shows that the steps in Chapters 1–3 can take up to half a day or more, and that a clear result is only just becoming apparent at the end of that. However, the outcome of these first three steps should be a more comprehensive and in-depth understanding of differing user needs, together with the first signs of groups of users, or segments, where the organisation can do more or better.

SUMMARY OF CHAPTERS 1–3

KEY ACTIONS	POINTS TO CONSIDER	REFERENCE
■ Market Map	■ The flow of goods to the final user	■ Figure 1.2
■ Market definition	■ The scope of your search for new opportunities	■ pp. 13–17
■ Market Audit	■ The current market position and key trends	■ Figure 1.3
■ Brainstorming	■ Who buys, what do they buy, and why?	■ Tables 2.1, 2.3 and 2.4

In Table 4.1, a simplified example of this type of quantitative approach is illustrated. In this example, growth and profitability are seen as the most important factors, and this is reflected in a slightly higher weighting for these two. Each segment is then scored against the criteria for each factor – as our example segment is valued at between £10 million–£19 million, and growing in excess of 10 per cent per annum, it therefore scores 5 and 10 respectively, and so on. Finally, the score is then multiplied by the percentage weighting to give a ranking. The higher the overall ranking (which in Table 4.1 is 6.0) the more attractive the segment is to the organisation.

At this stage, it is acceptable to adjust some of the scoring criteria or weightings to reflect what you feel is a more accurate overall picture but, once adjusted, they should remain fixed for any subsequent segments you consider. However, when changes are made simply to boost the results of low-ranking segments, the analysis will obviously lose some of its value. Similarly, the quality of the analysis will be enhanced by quantitative scoring criteria, derived from market research, in preference to broad divisions of internal opinion such as low, medium and high.

JUDGING SEGMENT FIT WITH BUSINESS STRENGTHS

Having established at the outset of this book that marketing is fundamentally a matching process – that of matching organisational strengths to user needs – it follows that you must now judge how well equipped you are to tackle each of the segments you have identified in Chapter 3.

In completing your analysis for Chapters 1–3, you will have noted the general needs of users in each of your segments. In the course of your Market Audit (see pages 17–19), you will also have developed an understanding of your relative strengths and weaknesses versus other competitors in each of the segments (see also pages 53–4). In addition, you will have analysed your own organisational goals and resources, and formed an impression of your capacity and desire to move into new areas. Thus, you will have developed an appreciation of what factors are critical for further success in the market.

A list of possible critical success factors is given below.

- Market share
- Your profitability
- Technical competence
- Image
- Distribution channels
- Product quality
- Service orientation
- Level of innovation
- Personal relationships
- Ability to change
- Cost base

In choosing the most appropriate factors it is important to use a realistic and objective assessment, and this means that, at some stage, some of the factors must be verified by user research. If your understanding of user needs developed in Chapters 1–3 has come from observation, now is the time to actually ask the user. Internal perceptions of user needs are rarely shown to tally with actual user needs, and often what the organisation sees as being important for success, may be seen only as a very basic 'qualifier' by the user. An actual example of this is illustrated in Table 4.2, where you can see that the top three priorities of target users (on a scale of 1–5, with

Table 4.2 User perceptions versus internal perceptions

Users	*Mean score*	*Internal*	*Mean score*
1 Product availability	*1.84*	1 Customer relationships	2.17
2 Reliability of delivery	*1.86*	2 Technical support/backup	2.22
3 Product quality	*1.86*	3 Ease of order placement	2.23
4 Ease of order placement	1.86	*4 Reliability of delivery*	*2.30*
5 Security of product supply	1.94	5 Response to competition	2.30
6 Customer relationships	1.97	6 Security of product supply	2.37
7 Technical support/backup	2.00	7 Customer communication	2.39
8 Complaint handling	2.16	*8 Product availability*	*2.57*
9 Quality of literature	2.17	9 Documentation	2.60
10 Customer communication	2.33	10 Customer service	2.61
11 Documentation	2.39	11 Complaint handling	2.61
12 Customer service	2.72	*12 Product quality*	*2.74*
13 Price	2.93	13 Price	2.76
14 Response to competition	2.98	14 Quality of literature	2.76

1 being the most important) are dangerously spread amongst those of internal personnel. Thus, it is recommended that third-party-collected, objective user research, should be considered for input to this stage.

Having selected the key success factors, it is then possible to conduct a quantitative analysis of your business's strengths, taking a similar approach to that used to determine segment attractiveness. In the example in Table 4.3, which is for a current segment, we can see that with an overall business strength score of 7.5 (10.0 being the maximum), this particular segment is one that the organisation is well qualified to develop. The analysis also indicates that the strengths of the business are the level of its product differentiation from its competitors, and thus its market share, and that quality is a possible improvement area. Again, in its purest form, the factors, scores and the weightings used to complete Table 4.3, should be quantified and reflect some input from user research.

Table 4.3 Business strengths evaluation

Factor	*10*	*5*	*0*	*Score*	*Weight*	*Rank*
1 Market share (%)	>25	10–24	<10	10	30	3.0
2 Profitability (%)	>15	10–14	<10	5	20	1.0
3 Differentiation	High	Medium	Low	10	30	3.0
4 Product quality	High	Medium	Low	0	10	0.0
5 Innovation level	High	Medium	Low	5	10	0.5
				TOTAL	100	7.5

MATCHING ATTRACTIVENESS TO STRENGTHS

Having identified the attractiveness of each of your possible segments, and determined your own ability to tackle them, you now need to develop an overall prioritisation before deciding on your plan of attack.

It is possible to illustrate your options with a simple four-box grid. In Figure 4.1 such a format is illustrated, with segment attractiveness on the vertical axis, and business strengths on the horizontal axis, and each axis numbered from 0 to 10. Using your

Figure 4.1: Portfolio Analysis

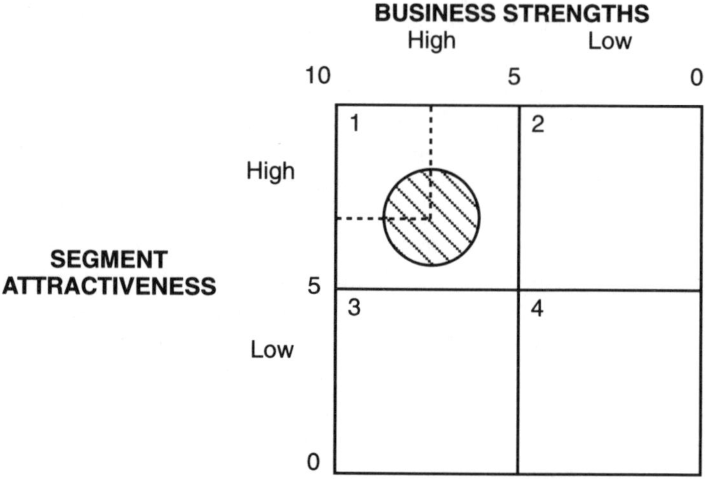

scores from Tables 4.1 and 4.3, you can then plot the segment, and subsequently all others under consideration, adopting a suitable scale for the diameter of the circle to indicate relative segment size.

It can be seen from Figure 4.1, that the example we have been using appears in the top left-hand box – an attractive segment, and one that we are well placed to enter or develop – and as such is a priority for management action. Segments appearing in box 2 are good opportunities, being relatively attractive ones, but would need further investment to improve your strength score. Any segments appearing in boxes 3 and 4 are consequently lesser opportunities, and the reasons for this would be clear from the Analysis you create in completing Tables 4.1 and 4.3. It is of course important to remember that segments in the lower half of the grid are simply lesser opportunities, and not necessarily unattractive.

It is also important to remember that the segments, and their scores, do not last forever. Thus you should consider how the segments are likely to fare over the planning period, before developing your plan for the 'winners' in the next chapter. This can be most simply done by inserting likely future values (typically those for the end of your planning period) into Tables 4.1 and 4.3, and drawing an additional circle (most likely of a different size) in your

Figure 4.2: Portfolio Analysis, year 3

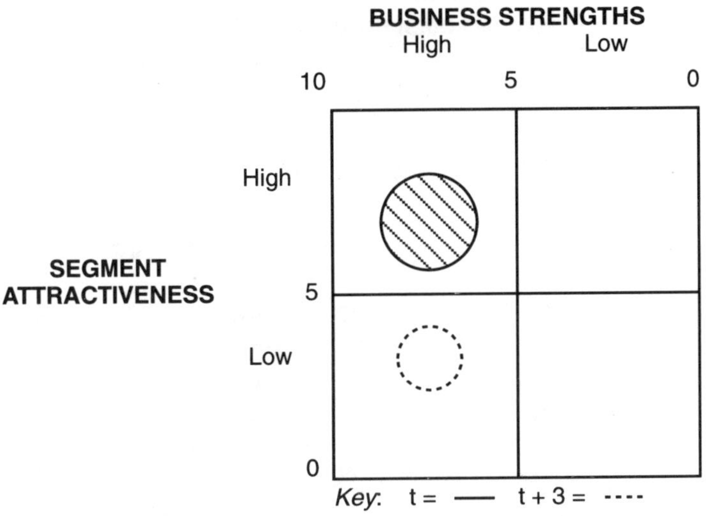

grid. In Figure 4.2, we can see that our example segment (as indicated by the dotted line circle) is hypothetically shown to become smaller and less attractive over the course of the planning period, and consequently not the opportunity we first thought. You could of course use just this forward-looking approach to prioritise your segments, but as it tends to involve a greater level of judgment, it would be wise to produce a current position analysis too (i.e. for year t), for comparison purposes.

This type of analysis thus has several advantages over other approaches to prioritising new business opportunities: first, it allows multiple factors to be considered, and in a quantifiable way, which makes for a more meaningful analysis; second, it is not just a situational analysis of one point in time, it can also accommodate likely future changes; and finally, it works equally well on both current segments and likely future ones, as well as on markets.

All too often though, this fourth step in the segmentation process is accorded little more than a cursory check (and usually then for attractiveness only), in an impatience to create something for the new opportunities that have been identified. With good information, the Analysis can be completed in less than half a day, and it does bring some objectivity to the task of deciding between different new business alternatives. More crucially, the approach helps to focus attention on the key areas where the organisation can make its competitive advantage tell.

Having completed your Portfolio Analysis, you are now ready to develop your plan of attack.

SUMMARY OF CHAPTERS 1–4

KEY ACTIONS	POINTS TO CONSIDER	REFERENCE
■ Market Map	■ The flow of goods to the final user	■ Figure 1.2
■ Market definition	■ The scope of your search for new opportunities	■ pp. 13–17
■ Market Audit	■ The current market position and key trends	■ Figure 1.3
■ Brainstorming	■ Who buys, what do they buy, and why?	■ Tables 2.1, 2.3 and 2.4
■ Screening	■ Relevant, substantial and accessible bases?	■ Table 3.1
■ Fishbone Technique	■ The precise needs or user groups for each base	■ Figures 3.1 and 3.2
■ Segment definition	■ Possible groupings of segmentation variables	■ Figure 3.3
■ **Using your list of definitions, develop a prioritised list of winning segments.**	■ **What is the relative attractiveness of each segment? How well equipped are you to succeed in them?**	■ **Tables 4.1 and 4.3, Figure 4.1**

5 *Developing the plan of attack*

Having selected the best segments to improve your competitive position, you can now begin to look at some of the different strategic choices you have, and what specifically you need to do to develop your offer to meet segment needs.

It is important to note however, that the process of market segmentation is not something that happens in isolation from other strategic planning activities. Indeed segmentation is an integral part of the marketing planning process. Having developed your understanding of the early stages of market segmentation, you are now well placed to look at how it should fit into your overall planning process.

SEGMENTATION AND THE MARKETING PLAN

Figure 5.1 illustrates the steps that must be gone through in order to arrive at a marketing plan. The process basically offers a logical and largely sequential approach, from initially a very broad perspective, down to the specifics of who will do what, and by when.

The apparent simplicity of the process should not fool you into thinking of it as a mechanical one, nor indeed a straightforward one. The theory of marketing planning is after all extensively documented (McDonald 1984), and therefore readily available to your competitors. What tends to distinguish good marketing planners from the also-rans, is a company-wide marketing orientation, quality information, plus a good measure of both creativity and vision.

Successful planning therefore requires a high level of skill in/

Figure 5.1: The marketing planning process

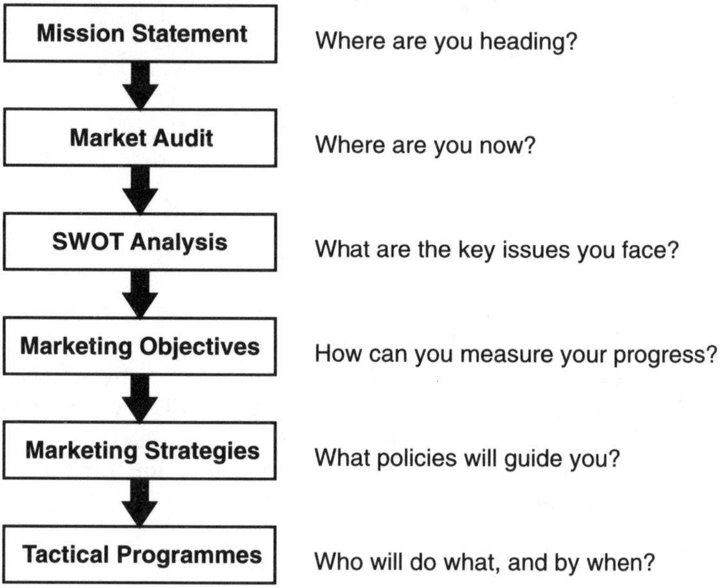

knowledge of/motivation towards marketing, in addition to a good process, and may not always come easily. However, you must persevere because the alternative is rather like a cork that is tossed around in a sea of competition: progress is unsteady and unreliable – just like it is for the poor old cork!

This approach to planning – moving from the broad to the specific – is similar to, and in fact dovetails, that which we have discussed for segmentation (see Figure 5.2). Moreover, the two approaches are interdependent: marketing planning becomes too diverse and unfocused without a segmented approach, and market segmentation can only be pursued after consideration of the many other issues facing the organisation.

The overall direction for the market segmentation process, should come from the organisation's Mission Statement. The Mission is an unquantified dream of the future – of what the organisation is striving to become and how – and it therefore communicates the purpose of the organisation, and provides guidance for decision makers. Specifically, and with relevance to segmentation, the Mission Statement should include:

- the role or contribution of the organisation – e.g. to maximize profits, or to provide a service;
- a definition of the business – i.e. what markets you are in and/or intend to be in;
- a statement of differentiation – i.e. the distinctive competence you have and/or intend to gain;
- an indication of future direction – i.e. things that you are striving to do or become.

The early stages of the segmentation process (Chapters 1–3) are best completed in conjunction with your Market Audit. The Audit is a situational analysis of where you are now, and involves a fundamental appraisal of the market and your position in it, in relation to users, competitors, and the general business environment (see also pages 13–17). We have already noted that the planning process is largely a sequential one, and that puts a significant emphasis on the need for good quality up to date information in the Audit stage – for if the same ideas go in the top of the process, the same old programmes tend to come out of the bottom. In other words, the process has a tendency to reinforce current internal thinking in the absence of up-to-date market information.

Thus the process of dividing up the market to identify groups of users who might require different products and/or promotions needs to be undertaken, and annually revisited, as part of your Market Audit (see also Figure 6.2).

The process of selecting attractive segments (Chapter 4) begins with the SWOT (strengths, weaknesses, opportunities, threats) Analysis. The SWOT Analysis is simply a summary of the Audit, and is an excellent tool for distilling the literally thousands of issues raised in the Audit, to a workable priority list of something in the order of thirty to forty key issues. Most organisations do SWOTs, because they are simple and fun to do, but few make the most of them as a strategic planning device.

The key to doing SWOTs is to focus on the differential strengths, weaknesses, etc. versus competition, for that is the key to finding ways to outperform them. Ignoring this relativity test

Figure 5.2: Segmentation and the marketing plan

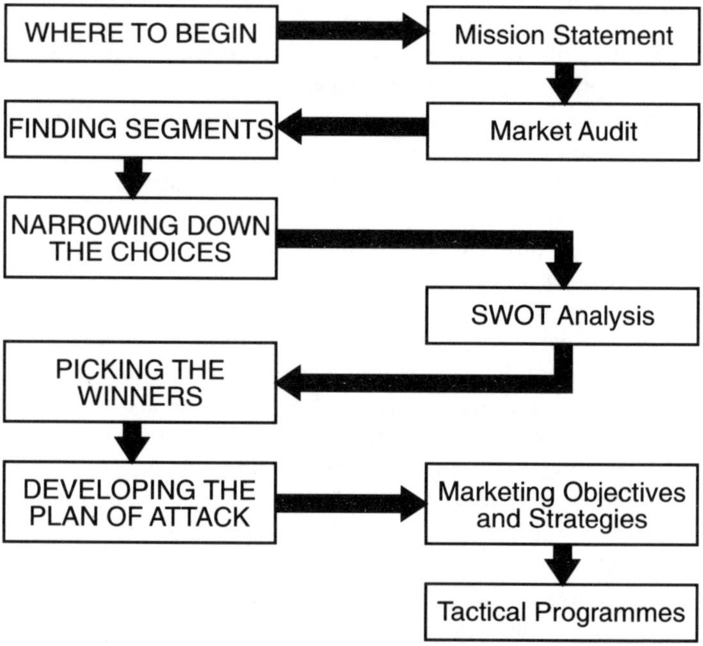

tends to lead to a long list of unrelated points that are difficult to action, and probably would not take the organisation that far forward, even if they were.

It is also important that SWOTs are only ever done on individual market segments, and never on the total business. An all encompassing SWOT tends to lead to a mass of averages, and then to strategies that are far too general, which in turn causes some specific opportunities to be glossed over. Thus the early steps of segmentation (see Chapters 1–3) must be completed before a SWOT analysis is tackled, and indeed your SWOT will form a major input to your Portfolio Analysis (see Chapter 4, pages 47–50).

Marketing Objectives are the quantifiable result of your planning activities i.e. what you want to achieve at the end of the planning period. Objectives should always be written around products and markets (i.e. the four broad options we noted in Figure 0.3), since it is only by selling something to somebody, that organisation can move forward and grow. Such market segmentation, with its identification and analysis of the best product and market options, plays an important part in establishing Marketing Objectives.

The final choice of which segments to attack to meet your Marketing Objectives, is part of strategy development and is the subject of the next section. The reader wishing to learn more of the subject of marketing planning, may like to consult the excellent publication – *Marketing Plans. How to Prepare Them: How to Use Them*, written by Malcolm H.B. McDonald, and published by Butterworth Heinemann (1984).

CONSIDERING YOUR STRATEGIC OPTIONS

With your list of winning segments developed in the last chapter, you are now in a position to choose how many segments to enter, and thus what overall strategy you will pursue. Essentially there are three broad strategic options, and Figure 5.3 illustrates these with a market for which four segments have passed the Portfolio Analysis.

An undifferentiated approach with the same product for all four

Figure 5.3: Market segments and the strategic options

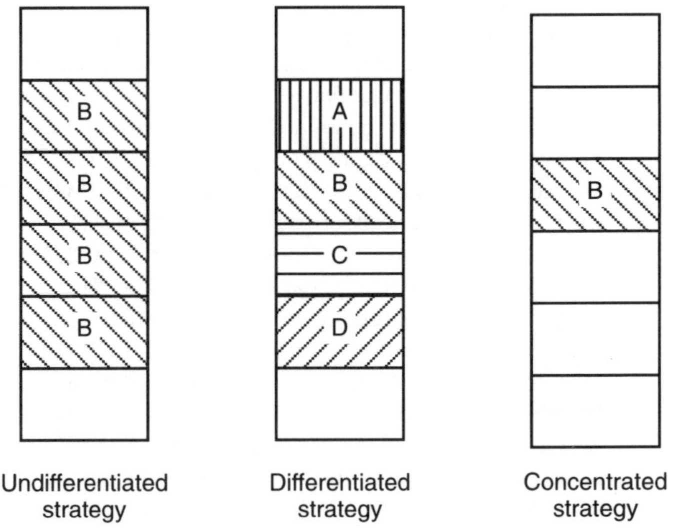

segments, for example one type of car for everyone, is the lowest unit cost route. This approach is suited to products that are highly innovative and/or have some form of legal protection, and to markets where user differences are slight. Thus an undifferentiated approach is often pursued in new markets, when marketing activity tends to be focused on getting the product right, and on telling everyone about it. In a new market situation, typically the offering is designed to appeal to the largest number of users, but even then this will very often cause the organisation to become a victim of its own success. As the new market grows, an undifferentiated approach will be more susceptible to competitive attack, especially in the more lucrative segments, and particularly if barriers to entry are low and/or user needs start to change.

Alternatively, you may consider a differentiated approach with a number of products/brands for each of a number of segments, for example a car for every purpose, purse and personality. Differentiation is most appropriate in mature markets where product differences are low, and whilst it is obviously a higher cost route, it tends to be the most secure.

For many organisations, faced with powerful competitors and relatively low resources, a concentrated approach, for example luxury cars, is more suited. However, a one-segment approach is particularly vulnerable to shifts in user needs and/or entry by a large competitor.

In terms of satisfying user needs and building competitive advantage, a differentiated approach is certainly the preferred option. However, faced with a number of segment choices where, for example, entry costs are high in terms of capital investment, you would be forgiven for leaning towards an undifferentiated (or shared cost) approach. It is important to note though, that the differentiated route need not extend to all aspects of the product offering. As we saw in Chapter 2 (see page 23), some aspects of the product – typically packaging and service – can have a big impact on user perceptions, whilst forming a relatively small part of total cost. In other words, it is possible to obtain some of the cost advantages of an undifferentiated approach, whilst benefiting from the competitive advantage that comes with differentiation.

The question of competition, also requires some further discussion. Obviously it makes sense to enter segments where there is little or no competition. Some indication of the level of compe-

Figure 5.4: A Perceptual Map of the holiday market

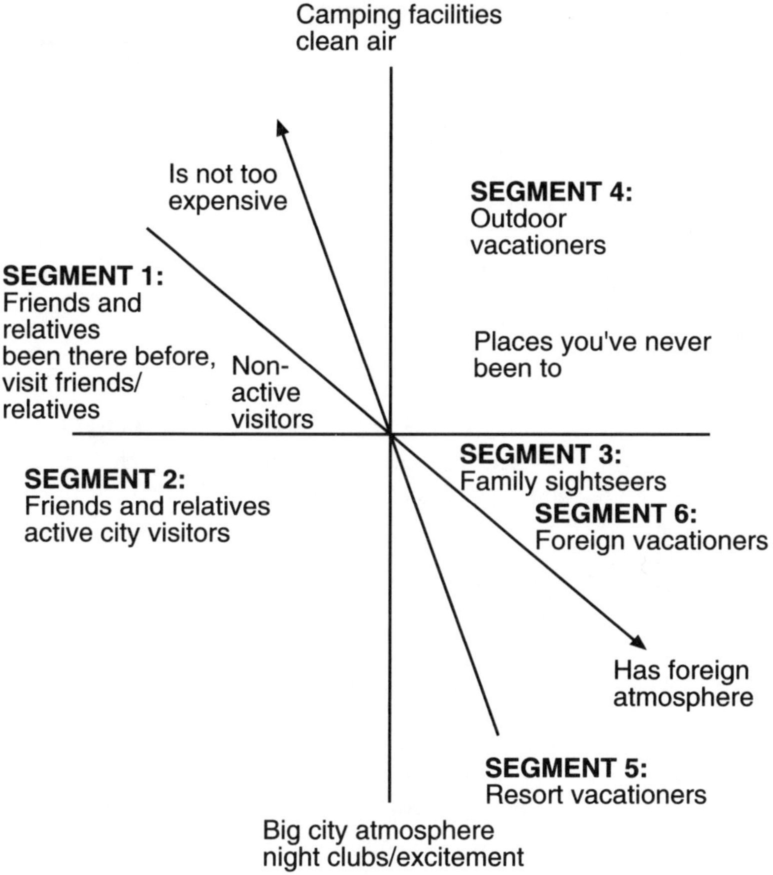

tition will usually have been gained in completing Table 4.1, however, this can be usefully supplemented by a Perceptual Map. In Figure 5.4, we can see a simplified example of this. Using your chosen segmentation variables and data collected in your Market Audit, you can plot key user groupings and competitors, thus identifying congested and sparsely populated areas. Lessig and Tollefson (1971) illustrate how a more sophisticated cluster analysis can help in completing such a Perceptual Map. This type of analysis is particularly helpful in determining your sequence of attack in your chosen segments. For example, when contemplating a number of segments in a new market, it clearly makes sense to target unserved areas first, followed by those on the fringe of competitor's strengths, so as to not provoke a response from incumbents who are likely to have a cost advantage.

Thus your choice of segments, and your sequence of attack, is dependent on a number of factors, many of which – segment size, level of competition, and so on – you will have considered in completing Tables 4.1 and 4.3. In addition, we have seen that it is important to make your decision after a final check on the resource and competitive interrelationships of all the winning segments you have identified.

DEVELOPING YOUR OFFER

Once final segments have been agreed, your next task is to develop your offer to meet the needs of your chosen segments. There are two important aspects to developing your offer:

- developing a product positioning for each segment
- developing a Marketing Mix for each segment

Product positioning

Product positioning involves presenting your product to fit a given place in the mind of the intended user. Your segment definition will have given you an indication of what is important to segment members. You now need to check the relative importance of each of the segmentation bases/variables and, if they concern a market in which you already operate, your rating on these variables versus competitors.

Measuring the relative importance of your segmentation criteria is best done by utilising trade-off techniques. The trade-off approach is based on the contention that users normally have to choose between a series of imperfect options, for example, the desire for product efficacy in a household cleaning agent will usually require the user to trade-off against some other desired quality, say 'gentleness' or 'greenness'.

Westwood, Lunn and Beazley (1979) have illustrated the trade-off approach as shown in Table 5.1. Here the respondent has been asked for a rank-order preference of the variables for two segmen-

Table 5.1 Trade-off Analysis

	Size of nearest town		
Position of hotel	*Fishing village*	*Major country town*	*Large city*
Facing the beach	1	2	5
5 minute walk to beach	3	4	8
More than 5 minute walk	6	7	9

Source: Westwood, Lunn and Beazley (1979)

tation bases that are appropriate to choosing a package tour holiday. The results indicate an overall preference for proximity to a fishing village and staying in a hotel facing the beach. Additionally, the results show a preference for staying near a major country town rather than having to walk to the beach, and walking to the beach rather than staying near a large city – providing the walk is less than 5 minutes, and so on.

Christopher (1992) shows that the simplified example in Table 5.1 can be expanded to include any number of segmentation bases and variables, and that by using computer analysis the implicit 'importance weights' that underlie the preferences can be generated. Thus it is possible to move beyond simply establishing the relative importance of, in our example, segmentation variables, to understanding how much the user is prepared to trade off one variable to get another.

From your Trade-off Analysis, you then need to understand (if it is a current segment) how your organisation fares against competition. This can be completed as part of a competitive benchmarking study, a simplified example of which is shown in Table 5.2. In such a study, decision makers from a representative sample of segment members, would be asked to rate competing suppliers according to the list of prioritised segmentation bases/variables you have created. Leppard and Molyneux (1994) illustrate how your study can also be usefully extended to include non-competing suppliers, in different markets, if they demonstrate excellence in overlapping user needs. Benchmarking thus reinforces the need for the all important twin focus of marketing – that of outperforming competitors at meeting the needs of users –

Table 5.2 Competitive benchmarking questionnaire

Q: How would you rate tyre manufacturer X on the following:

Tyre life	1	2	3	4	5
Safety	1	2	3	4	5
Ride quality	1	2	3	4	5
Price	1	2	3	4	5
Availability	1	2	3	4	5

Note: Score from 1–5: 1 = excellent, 5 = very poor

by indicating why the best are best, and what you have to do to overtake them.

The results of both your Trade-off Analysis and your benchmarking exercise (for a more detailed example output, see Table 4.2), can then be incorporated into a Performance Matrix as shown in Figure 5.5. In interpreting the Matrix, it is clearly crucial that you should aim to perform well in the areas that the user

Figure 5.5: A Performance Matrix for car tyres

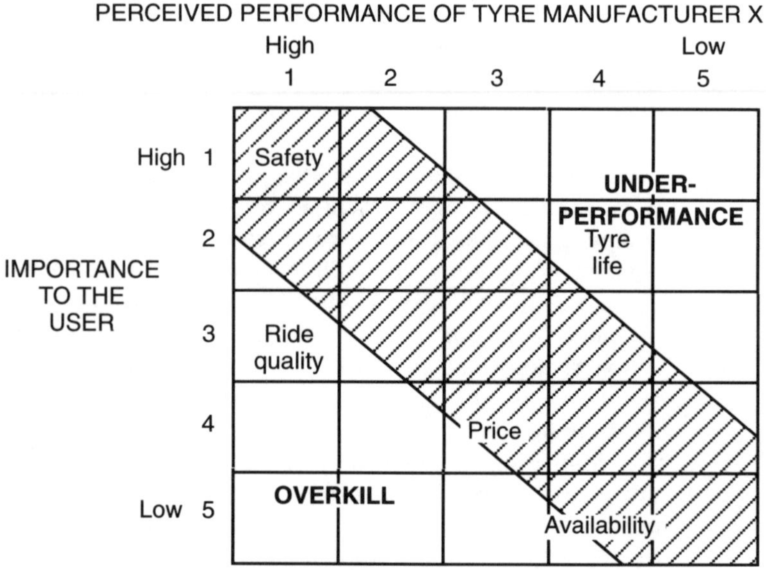

Figure 5.6: A Brand Positioning Map

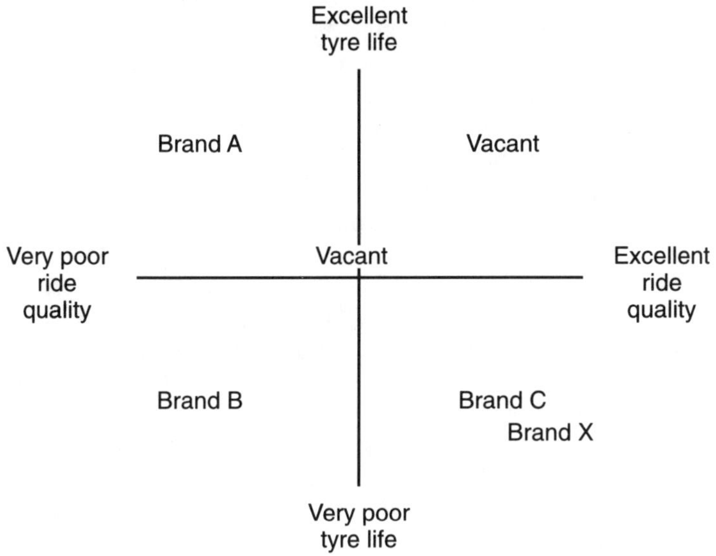

deems to be important. Equally, if a segmentation base/variable is seen to be less important to the user, then arguably a high performance amounts to a misuse of resources. Thus, you can start to think in terms of an imaginary diagonal band (as shown in Figure 5.5), which indicates the optimum level of performance for each base/variable, and how far away from it you are.

Additionally, it is possible to illustrate graphically your final positioning options by means of a Brand Positioning Map, and in Figure 5.6 we can see an example of one which focuses on the key 'ride quality/tyre life' segment. Our Performance Matrix has already indicated a possible sacrificing of ride quality to gain improved tyre life, for the current brand, and the Brand Map also highlights an additional opportunity for a premium product. Your final product positioning will thus be dependent on the size and location of preference clusters in the segment, and the proximity of competitive brands.

The Marketing Mix

Having now determined your final product positioning, you can start to think in terms of incorporating the benefits sought by the user group into your offer, and in such a way as to build competitive advantage. The 'tools' available to you to achieve this are known as the Marketing Mix – and sometimes referred to as the four Ps of marketing – your product, price, promotion and place (or distribution) decisions. Some organisations, typically service companies, like to add fifth and sixth Ps – processes and people – and certainly 'people' are an important, and all too often forgotten, resource.

Some examples of typical Marketing Mix decisions are shown in Table 5.3. These decisions will become your Marketing Strategies (see page 53), and thus describe how, in broad terms, you plan to meet your Marketing Objectives, i.e. what policies you plan to pursue. The content of your Strategies should reflect the issues noted in your segment SWOT Analysis (see page 53), and should focus on building on your strengths, eliminating your weaknesses, etc., so as to develop competitive advantage, and ideally an 'improved' SWOT 12 months on. One thing that of course should be clear, is that different segments will require a different 'mix' of decisions.

In the course of working through the segmentation process you will have developed a wealth of knowledge on users in your chosen segments. To help develop your Marketing Strategies, you should (using your segment definitions and the knowledge gained in

Table 5.3 Marketing Mix decisions

PRODUCT	the policies for product modifications and deletions, new products, positioning, packaging, design, branding etc.
PRICE	the pricing, discount and rebate policies to be followed for different product groups, in different segments
PLACE	the policies for distribution channels, inventory and customer service levels
PROMOTION	the policies for communicating with users through the sales force, advertising, direct mail, public relations, and so on.

Table 5.4 Toothpaste market segmentation

	Sensory segment	*Sociables*	*Worriers*	*Independent segment*
Benefits sought	flavour, product appearance	brightness of teeth	decay prevention	price
Demographic strengths	children	young people	large families	men
Behaviour	users of spearmint flavour	smokers	heavy users	heavy users
Brands favoured	Colgate Stripe	Macleans Ultra Bright	Crest	brands on sale
Personality	high self-involvement	high sociability	high hypo-chondriasis	high autonomy
Lifestyle	hedonistic	active	conservative	value orientated

Source: Haley (1968)

determining the optimal positioning of your product offer), expand your description of the segments, along the lines shown in Table 5.4. In this example, Haley (1968) illustrates an approach to segmentation based on benefits sought, with the corresponding demographic and psychographic characteristics associated with each of four segments.

Having completed your own version of Table 5.4 (albeit with different criteria in the left-hand column), it should be clear how this knowledge translates into product formulations, packaging policies, promotional policies, and so on. For example, Aquafresh toothpaste was subsequently developed to attract both the 'Sociables' and 'Worriers' in Table 5.4. Once your Marketing Mix decisions have been taken, you can now move into the final tactical phase of your marketing plan and the segmentation process. In short, all you need now do, is to develop a product/reposition a current one, that incorporates the particular benefits you have identified, and target a message to the segment seeking those benefits.

SUMMARY OF CHAPTERS 1–5

KEY ACTIONS	POINTS TO CONSIDER	REFERENCE
■ Market Map	■ The flow of goods to the final user	■ Figure 1.2
■ Market definition	■ The scope of your search for new opportunities	■ pp. 13–17
■ Market Audit	■ The current market position and key trends	■ Figure 1.3
■ Brainstorming	■ Who buys, what do they buy, and why?	■ Tables 2.1, 2.3 and 2.4
■ Screening	■ Relevant, substantial and accessible bases?	■ Table 3.1
■ Fishbone Technique	■ The precise needs or user groups for each base	■ Figures 3.1 and 3.2
■ Segment definition	■ Possible groupings of segmentation variables	■ Figure 3.3
■ Portfolio Analysis	■ Matching segment attractiveness to your business's strengths	■ Tables 4.1 and 4.3, Figure 4.1

KEY ACTIONS	POINTS TO CONSIDER	REFERENCE
■ **Illustrate your different segment options on a Perceptual Map.**	■ **Consider the cost and competitive interrelationships of the segments, before deciding on your final choice and sequence of attack.**	■ **Figure 5.4**
■ **Using user research, develop a Performance Matrix and Positioning Map for each of your chosen segments.**	■ **What are perceived to be the key segmentation variables, and how are you faring against competition on each?**	■ **Figures 5.5 and 5.6**
■ **Write some strategy statements for each of your segments, under the headings of the 4 Ps of the Marketing Mix.**	■ **How, in broad terms, are you aiming to achieve your objectives for each segment? How can you maximise your competitive advantage, and build added value into your offer?**	■ **Table 5.3**

6 *Staying ahead*

It should be clear from all that we have discussed on the concept of market segmentation that the process should not end once a product has been identified and launched. Indeed, there are two final stages you should consider:

- organising around your chosen segments
- monitoring/reviewing your segmentation strategies

ORGANISING TO SUCCEED

We have already noted that one of the key criteria for effective segmentation is 'fit' with business strengths. It follows from this that a business that organises around its chosen segments, will be more responsive than one organised around functions, or products, or geographical areas.

All too often organisations, having followed a market-led approach to analysing business opportunities, fail to then apply the same focus to the structure and the culture of their organisation. If you maintain a functional or product-orientated structure, it is inevitable that your new-found market focus will be dulled with time. In the extreme, key parts of your organisation will be unaware that certain segments are being targeted and, more crucially, unaware of the needs of those segments.

Schein (1985) suggests that most corporate structures are largely backward looking, in the sense that they have evolved around what tended to work in the past – as the market around them changes, they too change, but only in an incremental way, and not at the same pace as the market. Creating a market-led organisation thus involves taking a forward-looking approach to identifying the dominant pattern of the segment, and the qualities required to compete effectively within it. Market segments can normally be characterized by one of four dominant growth patterns:

- New segment – very unstable
- Established segment – with strong growth
- Stable segment – plateaued growth
- Declining segment

Having identified the dominant pattern, you should then create a Strategic Business Unit (SBU) that embodies the essential qualities of the segment. For example, it would clearly be inappropriate in a new segment, to adopt a rigid hierarchical structure, that was designed to minimise initiative, that had an over-insistence on procedures, and that had a reward system that encouraged compliance.

An SBU is a separate and identifiable unit, with a manager who has authority for most of the key decisions that are critical to success in the segment. Exactly how far you go in terms of developing an organisational structure along SBU lines, will depend on the number of markets you operate in, and the size and number of segments you have identified. Your Segment Tree (see Figure 3.3, page 40) will give you the best indication of your options, and you could choose to develop SBUs around markets (or industry group, as in Figure 3.3), or segments, or even subsegments. However, having identified a number of homogeneous user groups – each group having different needs and requiring different marketing approaches – the customer orientation of your organisation can only benefit from such a market-focused structure (see Figure 6.1).

More traditional structures – functional, geographic, product orientated, and so on – do have their merits, but they also tend to make the organisation more introspective in its outlook, and less proactive in terms of satisfying current and future customer needs. Sooner or later, companies adopting these traditional approaches will suffer from market shock – either through a shift in user needs, or through a change in strategy by a competitor. Sadly, these companies are then forced to reappraise the structure and culture of their organisation from a position of declining or maturing sales.

Figure 6.1: Moving to a market-focused organisation

a) Functional organisation

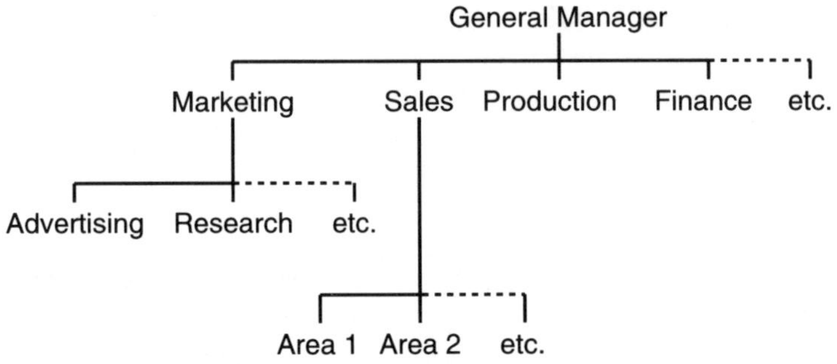

b) Product organisation

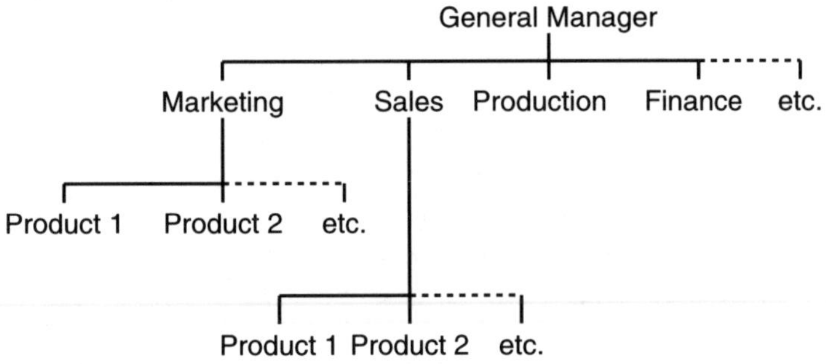

c) Market organisation

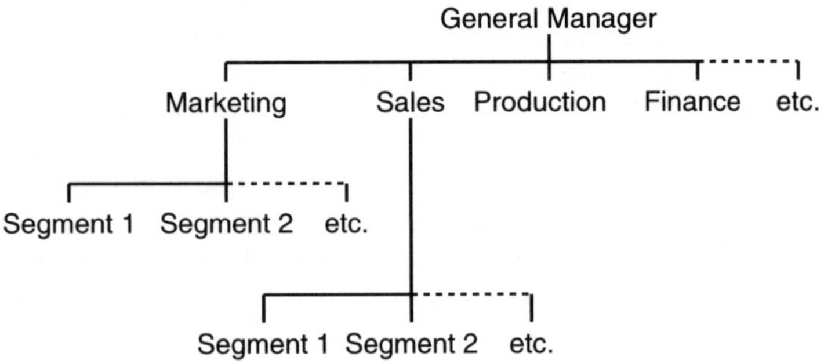

Sometimes companies respond with a variety of customer care programmes, but the effect of these is unlikely to be sustained without a corresponding change in structure as employees will gradually reorientate to their previous ways. The answer is to organise around customer groupings, and to do so from a position of market strength.

The final choice of the number and type of SBUs will also be influenced by organisational resources, as well as the cost inter-relationships between markets and/or segments. The style and timing of any change will similarly be influenced by personnel sensitivities. Certainly, a move away from a purely functional or product-orientated structure is best achieved in stages, and in this respect Figure 6.1(c) – tackling the Marketing and Sales Departments first – is a route that has worked well in a number of organisations.

Once SBUs are in place, they should then be managed as a portfolio (see pages 47–50), and in this way you can be sure that your market-led focus is preserved for future decisions on strategy and resource allocation.

MONITORING YOUR PROGRESS

It is equally important to remember that what you set in place, as a result of working through this segmentation process, will not last forever. The rigorous process you have now followed will certainly lead you to a position of strength in the market-place. However, user needs and preferences do change, and the programmes you develop as a result of market segmentation will have an impact on users, as well as on the activities of competitors. Thus the process of market segmentation needs to be an ongoing one.

Specifically, you need to establish the systems and procedures to collect information and to monitor your market-place performance, and this needs to be timetabled in line with your normal planning activities. This is best done by making your review a part of your Market Audit (see Figure 6.2). Such a review, which would fit easily under the headings we discussed in Figure 1.3 (see page 18), might include:

- Are we building stronger partnerships with customers, by improving their perception of our performance and service levels?

- Have we increased our market share and profit?
- How have competitors reacted in their marketing strategies?
- Has there been any noticeable shift in user needs as a result of our actions, or competitors' actions, or because of environmental influences?

Successfully monitoring, and indeed implementing, a segmented approach also relies heavily on adequate accounting information. Clearly, pursuing a variety of segments with only aggregate accounting information is at best half-hearted, and at worst will lead to a wastage of resources.

Busby and Heitger (1976) note that each segment's Marketing Mix (see pages 161–4) should be translated into cost and revenue implications, and then aggregated to give your organisation its overall targets. The segment targets will become your Marketing

Figure 6.2: Reviewing your progress

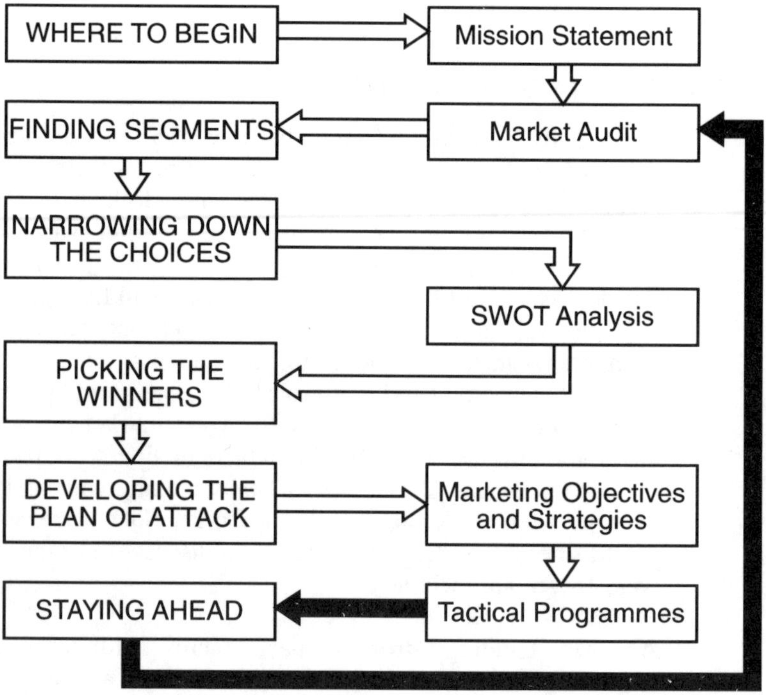

Objectives (see page 54), and will thus provide you with a quantifiable measure of your progress. It is of course important though, that reporting systems are altered to reflect your new focus. Additionally your Marketing Objectives will provide a more powerful yardstick under a market-focused structure, where individuals and departments are targeted and rewarded more directly on the basis of their contribution to market goals.

This final step in the segmentation process needs to be a pro-active one and a disciplined one, and obviously not a knee-jerk reaction to some planning deadline. When segmentation becomes a regular aspect of your planning cycle and reporting systems, market changes can be swiftly identified and acted upon, thus ensuring that you do in fact 'stay ahead'.

SUMMARY OF CHAPTERS 1–6

KEY ACTIONS	POINTS TO CONSIDER	REFERENCE
■ Market Map	■ The flow of goods to the final user	■ Figure 1.2
■ Market definition	■ The scope of your search for new opportunities	■ pp. 13–17
■ Market Audit	■ The current market position and key trends	■ Figure 1.3
■ Brainstorming	■ Who buys, what do they buy, and why?	■ Tables 2.1, 2.3 and 2.4
■ Screening	■ Relevant, substantial and accessible bases?	■ Table 3.1
■ Fishbone Technique	■ The precise needs or user groups for each base	■ Figures 3.1 and 3.2
■ Segment definition	■ Possible groupings of segmentation variables	■ Figure 3.3

KEY ACTIONS	POINTS TO CONSIDER	REFERENCE
■ Portfolio Analysis	■ Matching segment attractiveness to your business's strengths	■ Tables 4.1 and 4.3, Figure 4.1
■ Perceptual Map	■ Segment cost and competitive interrelationships, and your sequence of attack.	■ Figure 5.4
■ Performance Matrix	■ Matching your performance to perceived user importance	■ Figures 5.5 and 5.6
■ Marketing Mix	■ Developing competitive advantage and added value	■ Table 5.3
■ Assess the suitability of your current organisational structure, in the light of your new-found market focus.	**■ Consider organisational resources and life cycle stage, the segment interrelationships, and any personal sensitivities**	**■ Figure 6.1**
■ Monitor and review your progress with the new initiatives you have now set in place, by making segmentation a regular aspect of your planning cycle.	**■ How are users' needs changing? How have competitors reacted? What has been the effect on your market share and profits, and on your perceived performance?**	**■ Figure 6.2**

Summary

In today's competitive markets, few organisations can survive by offering one product to all users. Ignoring differences between users will mean specific opportunities for greater customer satisfaction are missed, but they may not be missed by your competitors. Ideally, you should think in terms of a different product and promotional message for every user, but seldom is this cost effective, or even possible, to consider.

Thus it makes sense to start to think in terms of groups of users who have similar needs. It also makes sense to focus on the groups that most closely fit your organisation's strengths, because that will make you less susceptible to competitive attack. This is the theory of market segmentation.

For *planning* purposes, market segmentation helps define:

- the needs and priorities of users, around which different strategies can be evaluated;
- the basis for matching organisational strengths to market opportunities
- who and what the precise nature of competition is, or may become;
- the basis for entry/exit decisions.

For *implementation* purposes, market segmentation helps:

- define the most appropriate Marketing Mix – your product, price, place and promotion decisions – to build competitive advantage;
- direct sales efforts to the most beneficial targets;
- give the organisation a greater customer orientation;
- monitor and track the results of marketing programmes.

In every market, there are opportunities awaiting those who apply market segmentation techniques. One example of a product that has recently extended a market to take in a large and previously unserved segment, is that of 'trainer pants'. Any parent will remember the difficult period between when nappies are first discarded and when the child is successfully trained. With hindsight it seems obvious that 2 to 3 year olds (and their parents!) would have the need for a form of nappy that could be easily removed by a child, and yet provides a safeguard against accidents. The need has always been there, but disposable nappies had been around for 20 years before the opportunity was realised.

In this book I have outlined a step-by-step guide that any organisation can use to take advantage of the concept of segmentation, to realise market opportunities. This process is repeated in summary form in Table S.1. I make no apology for the involved nature of the approach, for if finding new business was easy, others would surely find it too.

Like any process though, it should not be viewed as a mechanical one that will in itself deliver profitable new business. Successful market segmentation is as much dependent on the quality of the market information you start with, and the creativity you apply in using that information, as it is to following the right process. In other words, your competitors will be reading this as well!

Table S.1 A step-by-step approach to market segmentation

CHAPTER	*KEY STEPS*
1 WHERE TO BEGIN	■ Define the market
	■ Understand the market
2 FINDING SEGMENTS	■ Explore user differences
3 NARROWING DOWN THE CHOICES	■ Refine the segmentation bases
	■ Identify the segmentation variables
	■ Define the segment(s)
4 PICKING THE WINNERS	■ Determine segment attractiveness and business strengths
5 DEVELOPING THE PLAN OF ATTACK	■ Consider the strategic options
	■ Develop a product positioning
	■ Develop the Marketing Mix
6 STAYING AHEAD	■ Organise to succeed
	■ Monitor your progress

KEY ACTIONS	*OUTCOMES*
■ Market Map Market definition	■ A definition of the market expressed in terms of the overall end-user need
■ Market Audit/ Overview	■ A detailed understanding of the market and your position in it
■ Brainstorming	■ A list of differences (or segmentation bases) between users who share the same overall need
■ Screening	■ A refined list of the most relevant, substantial and accessible bases
■ Fishbone Technique Segment Matrix	■ An understanding of the precise user groups and their needs
■ Segment Tree Segment definition	■ A segment definition expressed in terms of a combination of segmentation bases and variables
■ Portfolio Analysis	■ A prioritised list of segments that are attractive/fit business strengths
■ Perceptual Map	■ An indication of how many segments to enter
■ Trade-off Analysis Benchmarking	■ A prioritised list of segmentation variables, with an indication of how you are faring against competition on each
■ Performance Matrix Positioning Map	■ An understanding of how best to position your product
■ Marketing Mix	■ A matching of benefits sought with those offered by you, that delivers sustainable competitive advantage
■ Structure ■ Marketing Planning Process	■ The structure and procedures to sustain your new-found market-led focus, and to monitor and review your segmentation strategies

Appendix

AN A–Z OF SEGMENTATION BASES WITH SOME TYPICAL VARIABLES

ATTITUDE	Hostile, negative, neutral, positive, enthusiastic
BENEFITS	Convenience, safety, low price, appearance, etc.
CLASS	Upper middle class (A), Middle class (B), Lower middle class (C1), Skilled working class (C2), Working class (D), Others (E)
DELIVERY	Same day, next day, 7 days, etc.
ETHNIC	White, ethnic minorities
FAMILY SIZE	0, 1, 2, 3, 4, 5, 6+ persons
GEOGRAPHIC	North Scotland, Central Scotland, Ulster, Border, North East, North West, Yorkshire, East and West Midlands, Wales and the West, East of England, London, South and South East, South West
HOUSING	Owner-occupied, owned outright, owner-occupied with mortgage, rented from local authority, rented, other

INCOME	£0–4,999; £5,000–14,999; £15,000–24,999; £25,000–49,999; £50,000–99,999; £100,000+
JOB	Senior management, professional, middle management, junior management, supervisory clerical, skilled workers, semi- and unskilled workers, retired, students, housewives and unemployed
KNOWLEDGE	Expert, competent, novice
LIFE CYCLE	Dependent, pre-family, family and empty nest
MARKETING	Sensitivity to advertising, sales promotion, service and price
NATIONALITY	British, American, Japanese, Chinese, etc.
OUTLET	Hardware shop, supermarket, petrol stations, direct mail, DIY shed, stationery shop, etc.
PERSONALITY	Sociable, unsociable, ambitious, conservative
QUANTITY	Singles, carton, parcel, pallet, container
READINESS	Unaware, aware, interested, desirous, about to buy
SEX	Male, female
TECHNOLOGY	Craft, mechanical, electro-mechanical, electronic
USER STATUS	User, non-user, potential user, lapsed user, new user, regular user, irregular user, loyal user, etc.
VOLUME	Light, medium and heavy users

WEALTH	Low income/high assets, high income/low assets, liquid assets, non-liquid assets, etc.
X	
YOUTH	Early teens, 16 plus, over 18
ZODIAC	Pisces, Libra, Scorpio, Aquarius, etc.

References

Abratt, R. (1993) 'Market Segmentation Practices of Industrial Marketers', *Industrial Marketing Management* 22: pp. 79–84.

Ansoff, H.I. (1957) 'Strategies for Diversification', *Harvard Business Review* September–October: pp. 113–24.

Baalbaki, I.B. and Malhotra, N.K. (1993) 'Marketing Management Bases for International Market Segmentation: An Alternate Look at the Standardization/Customization Debate', *International Marketing Review* 10, 1: pp. 19–44.

Busby, S.L. and Heitger L.E. (1976) 'Profit Orientated Reporting for Marketing Decision Makers', *MSU Business Topics* 24, 3 pp. 20–44.

Christopher, M. (1992) *Logistics and Supply Chain Management*, London: Pitmans.

De Kluyver, C.A. and Whitlark, D.B. (1986) 'Benefit Segmentation for Industrial Products', *Industrial Marketing Management* 15: pp. 273–86.

Dickson, P.R. and Ginter, J.L. (1987) 'Market segmentation,
Product Differentiation, and Marketing Strategy', *Journal of Marketing* 51: pp. 1–10.

Doyle, P. and Saunders, J. (1985) 'Market Segmentation and Positioning in Specialized Industrial Markets', *Journal of Marketing* 49 (Spring): pp. 24–32.

Engle, J.F., Fiorello, H.F. and Cayley, M.A. (1972) *Market Segmentation*, New York: Holt, Rinehart and Winston, Inc.

Haley, R.J. (1968) 'Benefit Segmentation: A Decision Orientated Research Tool', *Journal of Marketing* July: pp. 30–5.

Kotler, P. (1976) *Marketing Management. Analysis, Planning and Control* (7th edn 1991), London: Prentice-Hall.

Leppard, J.W. and Molyneux, E. (1994) *Auditing your Customer Service*, London: Routledge.

Lessig, V.P. and Tollefson, J.O. (1971) 'Market Segmentation Through Numerical Taxonomy', *Journal of Marketing Research* 8: pp. 480–87.

Majaro, S. (1988) *The Creative Gap*, London: Longman.

McDonald, M.H.B. (1984) *Marketing Plans. How to prepare them: How to use them* (2nd edn 1989), Oxford: Butterworth-Heinemann.

McDonald, M.H.B. and Leppard, J.W. (1991) *The Marketing Audit. Translating Marketing Theory into Practice*, Oxford: Butterworth-Heinemann.

Plank, R.E. (1984) 'A Critical Revue of Industrial Market Segmentation', *Industrial Marketing Management* 14, 2: pp. 79–91.

Robertson, T.S. (1971) *Innovative Behaviour and Communications*, New York: Holt, Rinehart and Winston, Inc.

Schein, E.H. (1985) *Organisation, Culture and Leadership*, New York: Jossey-Bass.

Shapiro, B.P. and Bonoma, T.V. (1984) 'How to Segment Industrial Markets' *Harvard Business Review* May–June: pp. 104–10.

Smith, W.R. (1956) 'Product Differentiation and Market Segmentation as Alternative Marketing Strategies', *Journal of Marketing* Vol. 21, July: pp. 3–8.

Thomas, R.J. and Wind, Y. (1982) 'Towards Empirical Generalizations in Industrial Market Segmentation', *Journal of Marketing* 43, 2: pp. 54–64.

Tull, D.S. and Hawkins, D.I. (1976) *Marketing Research – Meaning, Measurement, and Method*, New York: Macmillan.

Westwood, R., Lunn, A. and Beazley, D. (1979) 'The Trade-Off Model and its Extensions', *Journal of The Market Research Society* 16, 3: pp. 227–41.

Wind, Y. and Cardoza, R. (1974) 'Industrial Market Segmentation', *Industrial Marketing Management* 3: pp. 153–66.

Wind, Y. and Douglas, S. (1972) 'International Market Segmentation', *European Journal of Marketing* 6, 1: pp. 17–25.

Yankelovich, D. (1964) 'New Criteria for Market Segmentation', *Harvard Business Review* March–April: pp. 83–90.